To my parents, who took me to every state. And to Craig and Bessie, with whom I love sharing suitcases, sleeping bags, sandwiches and stories. — G.L.

For Eddy and Patti, who are already on the way to being truly great cooks and adventurous travellers. — J.B.

To William, Georgia, Charlie, and Alice who always keep our kitchen alive and buzzing. You are my inspiration for constant culinary creation. — D.L.A.

GRATITUDE IS DUE:

To my delightful publisher, Cecily Kaiser; art director, Meagan Bennett; and editor, Ellen Morrissey, who made this project so much fun that it did not feel like work at all. And to Emily Takoudes, who started the whole thing.

To Rachel Faber-Machacha, Fiona McBride, Julie Cooper, and Kristin Donnelly, dear friends who helped me make this book and allowed me to mix business, pleasure, wild salmon, and coconut salad. Rachel, you made me laugh out loud so many times.

To my husband, who literally brings home the bacon (and is tied with my dad for being the most patient person in the world): you are always willing to slam on the brakes for crab cakes, and occasionally ate things like caldo verde and sour cream raisin pie while I worked on this book, but also often ate cereal for supper while I typed. Craig, I am glad we had those two dozen oysters on our first date, and look forward to many more before we're done.

To my parents, who took our family across America and back again—Alaska, Hawaii, Maine, Florida, and everywhere in between—and taught me to read, write, and cook, starting with my very first recipe: toast. To my brother and sister, who rode in the back seat with me on endless hours of family road trips and along the way shared fry bread tacos, scallop ceviche, venison roadkill, wild pawpaw, roadside barbecue, and a few other things that are more meaningful than food.

To my daughter's friends, including Kiran, Mimi, Lilia and Junie, who taught me about being nine.

And to my daughter, who is always ready for a red-eye flight, a long drive, or a mango lassi, who was essential in the writing of this book, and whom I once considered naming "America." Bessie, where should we go next?

-G.L.

United Tastes of America

BY **GABRIELLE LANGHOLTZ**

WITH DRAWINGS BY **JENNY BOWERS** AND PHOTOS BY **DL ACKEN**

TABLE OF CONTENTS

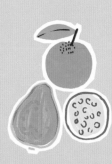

Dear Reader,

If someone from another country asked you to describe American food, what would you say? You might answer that Americans love hot dogs, hamburgers, and pizza. It's true, those dishes are popular, from coast to coast. But they're not the whole American menu—not by a long shot!

When I was your age, my family traveled to many different parts of the country. I soon realized that each place had its own tastes, and I was interested in them all! Up in New England, I imitated the locals and ordered lobster rolls. Down in Maryland, I learned why everyone craves crab. On Florida's beaches, I ate sea snail salad and Key lime pie. In Texas ranch country, I had tacos for breakfast and barbecued brisket for lunch. Out in California, I feasted on artichokes and avocados. And up in Alaska, I tasted fiddlehead ferns and wild salmon.

Some state favorites are based on local harvests, like Jersey tomatoes, Georgia peaches, Wisconsin cheese, New Mexico's chile peppers, Puerto Rican pomelo, Mississippi catfish, Michigan's wild rice, and Oregon's oysters.

Other regional foods reflect history, like the beef you'll find in Chicago, from when the city's stockyards provided much of America's meat…Or the apple orchards across Ohio, started from seeds planted by Johnny Appleseed himself… Or the cowboy beans still simmered over campfires in Colorado…Or the traditional tacos in Southern California, from the days when it was still part of Mexico.

Still, other local recipes can tell you who lives in a place. Immigrants have been coming to America for hundreds of years, and they've brought recipes from around the world. That's why you'll find Swedish meatballs in Minnesota,

Polish pierogies in Illinois, African peanut soup in Virginia, Cajun gumbo in Louisiana, Cuban sandwiches in Florida, and Ethiopian injera in Washington, DC. It may surprise you to learn that, many of the foods we think of as the most American were brought here from other countries! You can thank German immigrants when you eat hamburgers and hot dogs, and Italians for bringing the pizza and pasta.

Now I'm grown-up with a daughter of my own, and there's nothing we love more than traveling and tasting, like I did when I was her age. After all, food is one of the best ways to learn about a place—its harvests, its history, and its people. Some of our favorite foods have been eaten by Native Americans for centuries: corn, beans, tomatoes, turkey, squash, and maple syrup. But we also love Japanese sushi, Indian curries, and purple Peruvian punch! America has been changing for hundreds of years, and you might say it gets a little more delicious every day.

So, whether you're going on a road trip—or want to eat your way around the country without leaving your kitchen— I hope this book will help you fall in love with our country's great big menu.

Dig in!

Gabrielle Langholtz

With every recipe, you'll see a series of circles indicating how challenging it is to cook. Many have only one circle filled in, suggesting they are easier than average; most have two circles filled in, and are of average difficulty; and a handful of recipes have three circles filled in, meaning that they are harder than average (and the most challenging in this book). Consider these ratings alongside your own experience level when deciding what to cook.

| **LEVEL OF DIFFICULTY** | **LEVEL OF DIFFICULTY** | **LEVEL OF DIFFICULTY** |
| ● ○ ○ | ● ● ○ | ● ● ● |

COOKING TIPS

Check in with a grown-up before you start cooking.
Make sure that there's someone close by who can help with any cooking or chopping, or in case you have questions.

Pay attention to the times given with each recipe to make sure you have enough time to see it through.
In most cases, there is no real way to "speed things up," and if you're new to cooking, it may take longer than noted.

Always read a recipe all the way through before you begin.
This way, you'll know which ingredients and equipment you need, and there won't be any surprises once you've already started cooking.

Measure carefully and accurately.
This makes a big difference, especially when you are learning to cook. (For more on measuring, see page 10.)

Clean your work surface as you go.
Wash your hands and tools well, especially after touching raw fish or meat, move dirty things to the sink or dishwasher, and wipe down the work surface as you move from one step to the next to avoid one big mess at the end.

Avoid throwing away good food.
You can often save bits of unused ingredients for other recipes.

Mind the heat!
Use heatproof mitts when handling food in and around the oven, and follow what the recipe says about heat levels.

Learn to use your senses.
Sometimes you may be able tell that something is done cooking by the way it looks, smells, sounds, feels, and of course, tastes. Recipes give you things to watch out for, but if you think that something is done before the time in the recipe, trust your instincts. Just make sure your meat, fish, and eggs are fully cooked.

Have fun!
The goal is not to make something that looks picture-perfect, but to be proud of your process, and, hopefully, to cook something delicious! Like most skills worth learning, cooking is all about practice. The more you cook, the more you will improve, and the more good things you will have to eat and share!

NINE TERMS TO KNOW

BOILING

You'll know a liquid is **boiling** when you see large bubbles bursting rapidly on its surface.

SIMMERING

Simmering happens just before boiling, when small bubbles just start to rise up to the surface of the cooking liquid. Often a recipe will ask you to bring something to a boil, and then turn it down to a simmer. In that case, lower the heat until you just see bubbles breaking on the surface.

STEAMING

Steaming is one way to cook vegetables with moist, gentle heat. Usually it involves using a steamer basket over simmering water in a pot with a tight-fitting lid.

BRAISING

Braising can happen on the stovetop or in the oven. When foods are braised, they are partially submerged in liquid and slowly cooked over low heat until deliciously tender.

PAN-FRYING

Pan-frying is just what it sounds like. Foods such as chicken, meat, or fish are cooked in a large skillet in a small amount of oil or butter until they are cooked through but still crisp.

GRILLING

Grilling means cooking over a live fire. This is almost always over metal grates, with charcoal or gas flames.

BROILING

Broiling is cooking directly under high heat in the oven. It's one way to get meats and vegetables to taste almost as good as those cooked outside on a backyard grill.

BAKING

When something is **baking**, the dry heat of the oven is cooking it. This is usually how breads, cakes, pies, cookies, and biscuits are made.

ROASTING

Roasting also occurs in the oven. The word is used for items like meats and vegetables.

COOKING HOW-TOS

HOW TO MEASURE

To **measure** liquids, use clear glass cups with spouts for pouring; make sure you're at eye level to the measuring line. For dry ingredients like sugar and flour, use graduated measuring cups with handles. Spoon the ingredients up and over the top, then use the flat side of a butter knife to level it off (work over a bowl as you do this). Smaller amounts of ingredients call for teaspoons and tablespoons. Fill the measuring spoons to the top, and then level them off.

HOW TO CHOP

In recipe instructions, ingredients are chopped to different sizes, ranging from "minced" to "coarsely chopped." **Minced** ingredients are the tiniest (about ⅛ inch big). Something that's **finely chopped** is in small (about ¼ inch) pieces. **Coarsely chopped** ingredients are larger, about ⅓ to ½ inch in size. If a recipe doesn't specify the size of the chop, then it's not that important—you can chop them finely or coarsely.

Make sure that your knife is sharp enough to cut; believe it or not, dull knives cause more kitchen accidents than sharp ones. That's because it takes more pressure to cut through something with a dull knife, and that can cause the knife to slip and cut where it shouldn't.

Always chop your ingredients on a sturdy cutting board—never directly on the countertop or on a wobbly plate.

HOW TO SEPARATE EGGS

To **separate** egg yolks from whites, start with cold eggs, which are easier to separate than room temperature ones. Crack an egg into a bowl, then, with a clean, cupped hand, gently scoop up the yolk, taking care not to break it, and let the egg white drip back into the bowl. Transfer the yolk to another clean bowl, or directly into the mixing bowl, depending on your recipe.

HOW TO MELT BUTTER

To **melt** butter, warm it in a saucepan over low heat and watch until no solid pieces remain. Or use a microwave: put butter in a microwave-safe bowl and heat, checking every 20 seconds or so until it's fully liquid.

HOW TO CREAM BUTTER AND SUGAR

To **cream** together butter and sugar, start with room-temperature butter. Leave it out on the counter for about an hour (you can speed this up by cutting or grating it into small pieces). Once the butter is soft enough to hold your finger's indentation when pressed, use an electric mixer to combine it with the sugar. When you can't see the individual granules of sugar anymore (three to five minutes), it's creamed!

HOW TO KNEAD DOUGH

To **knead** bread dough, first lightly flour your hands and your work surface. The dough may be sticky at first, but the more you fold it over on itself, the less sticky it will be. Keep kneading, folding the dough over and onto itself and pushing it away with the heels of your hands until it starts to feel smooth. This can take about 10 minutes, so be patient! You may have to flour your hands or the surface again as you knead; be careful not to add too much (this can make your bread turn out tough).

HOW TO FOLD IN AN INGREDIENT

To **fold** one ingredient into another, you want to avoid overworking and deflating the batter. Add in the ingredient and then use a flexible spatula to work it in, making a letter *J* shape and gently flipping the batter up and over the new ingredient and turning the bowl as you go. Repeat this motion just until you no longer see the two separate ingredients.

HOW TO PREPARE PANS

To **prepare pans** for baking, first brush or rub the bottom and sides with softened butter. Then, "dust" them with flour: place about a teaspoon of flour in the pan and shake it all around the pan until it's covered (work over the sink, to avoid a mess!). This should keep your cake from sticking to the pan. Instead of flour, you can use parchment paper, cut into the same size as the bottom of the pan.

HOW TO USE SPICES AND SEASONINGS

Throughout this book, you will find recipes with black pepper, chile peppers (including jalapeños), fresh herbs, and ground spices. They are often listed as "optional," so you can leave them out if you wish. But each helps to broaden your palate and introduce you to new flavors and ingredients. If you are worried that something might be too spicy, start with a small amount and see if you like it. You can always work your way up to the full amount from there. (This is true for salt, too: start with a pinch and increase it only in small additions. Avoid adding too much salt.) Remember, the whole reason that people add these ingredients is that they are delicious!

When handling fresh chile peppers, you might want to remove the seeds and ribs first (they're the spiciest bits). Do avoid touching your mouth or eyes while you are chopping. And don't forget to wash your hands well afterward to remove any traces of heat!

Fresh herbs are sold in bunches. Some recipes will call for a "sprig," which means one whole stem and the leaves attached to it. Some herbs, like parsley and cilantro, have soft, tasty stems that you can include when you chop. But for most herbs, like basil, rosemary, mint, and thyme, pinch off the leaves to cook with, and discard the stems.

KITCHEN TOOLS

Cutting Board

Graters

Knives

Measuring Cups

Measuring Spoons

Mixer

Mixing Bowls

Rectangular Baking Dish

Rimmed Baking Sheet

Rolling Pin

Saucepan

Skillet or Frying Pan

Spatula

Stockpot

Tongs

Vegetable Peeler

Wire Rack

Whisk

Wooden Spoon

Cutting boards are made of plastic or wood, sometimes with slip-proof rubber dots on the bottom. For food safety reasons, it's best to keep one cutting board just for raw meat. For flavor reasons, keep another just for onions and garlic.

Graters come in box-style (these have four sides, with large and small holes) and rasp-style (with tiny teeth, for removing the rind [zest] from lemons and other citrus; it's also called a microplane grater)

Knives, including one 8- or 10-inch chef's knife and one small paring knife

Measuring cups, including one set of dry measuring cups in the standard sizes (¼, ⅓, ½, and 1 cup) and one clear glass liquid measuring cup with a spout for pouring (2 cups is a good all-purpose size)

Measuring spoons in the standard sizes (⅛, ¼, ½, and 1 teaspoon, and 1 tablespoon)

Mixer, either a standing electric mixer that sits out on the counter or a handheld model that can be easily stored in a drawer

Mixing bowls, made of metal or tempered glass (Pyrex), in small, medium, and large sizes

Rectangular baking dish (13 by 9 inches is most common and practical size)

Rimmed baking sheets, for baking cookies as well as roasting vegetables and meats

Rolling pin, for pie crusts and other doughs

Saucepan, in a medium (2-quart) size with a well-attached handle and tight-fitting lid

Skillet or frying pan, in a standard (8- or 10-inch) size, with a sturdy handle that's safe to put in the oven, too (cast-iron is a good choice)

Spatula, heatproof and flexible, for scraping every last bit of batter from a bowl or pan

Stockpot, with a tight-fitting lid, for boiling water for pasta and for making soup (12 quarts is a good size)

Tongs, with a handle that locks, for all kinds of kitchen tasks

Vegetable peeler, for peeling vegetables, shaving hard cheeses, and making chocolate curls

Whisk, for blending salad dressings, sauces, and more

Wire rack, for resting hot pans and baking sheets once they're removed from the oven and allowing cookies and cakes to cool after baking

Wooden spoons, for mixing just about everything

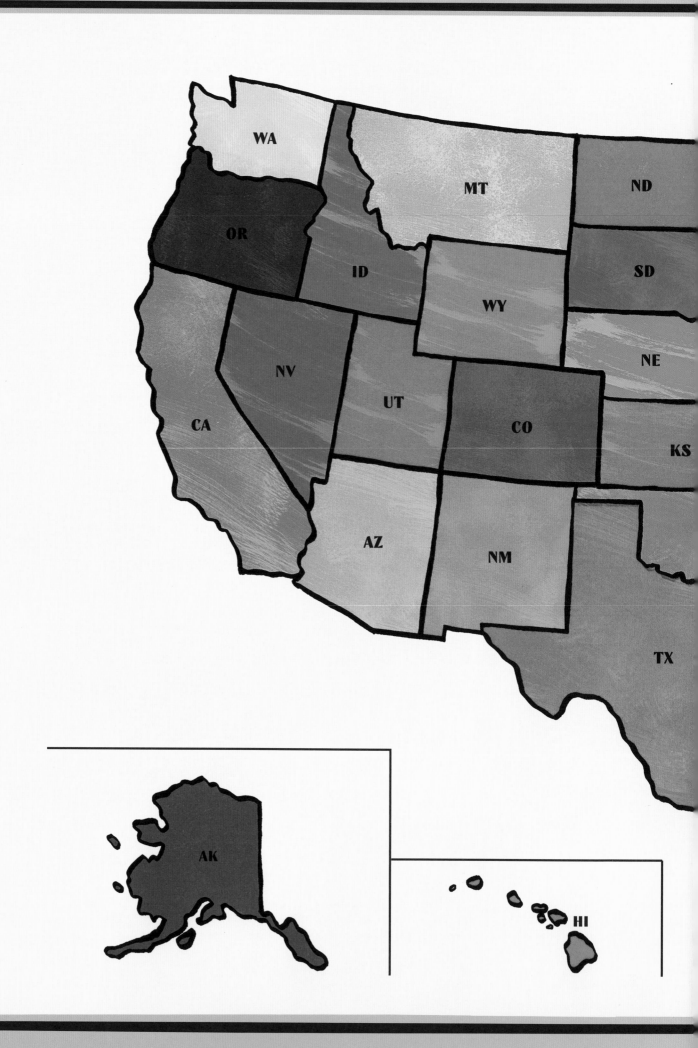

UNITED
STATES
of
AMERICA

Eating in ALABAMA

Food is an important part of creating community in Alabama. It might be smoked ribs in your neighbor's backyard, barbecue at a tailgate party in Tuscaloosa, or coconut meringue pie at a family reunion. Some Alabamans even celebrate "Decoration Day" every spring by cleaning up family grave sites while sharing picnics and memories right in the cemetery.

Many Alabama cooks fed the community during the civil rights movement of the 1950s and 60s. In 1955, after an African-American woman named Rosa Parks refused to give up her bus seat to a white man, she was arrested, which inspired the Montgomery bus boycott. Some African-American women sold fried chicken, sweet potato pies, and pound cakes, and gave the money to help boycotters pay for taxi rides. During the voting rights marches of 1965, social activists such as Dr. Martin Luther King, Jr., needed places to meet—and eat. Home cooks helped by hosting groups, and served biscuits, fried chicken, turnip greens, and black-eyed peas. These kitchens helped fuel a movement that made history. Today, you can still enjoy all these foods in Alabama and remember the brave cooks who strengthened their communities, one plate at a time.

WHITE BARBECUE SAUCE

Barbecue sauce in Alabama isn't red or brown—it's white! The simple mixture of mayonnaise, vinegar, and tons of black pepper is especially popular on chicken.

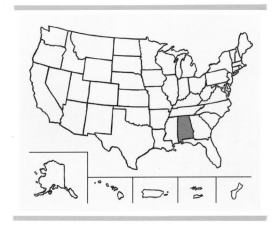

LANE CAKE

The official state dessert is Lane Cake, a white layer cake with nuts and dried fruits, covered in shiny frosting.

MONTGOMERY ★

FRIED GREEN TOMATOES

This popular dish is made by coating unripe tomato slices in cornmeal and frying them in hot oil.

WILD TURKEY

Alabama has more wild turkeys than any other state in the Southeast. They are often hunted and cooked!

PEANUTS

An Alabaman man named George Washington Carver was born into slavery but grew up to be a botanist and inventor. He found hundreds of uses for peanuts.

Peel-and-Eat Gulf Shrimp with Lemon-Garlic Butter

PREPARATION TIME	COOKING TIME	LEVEL OF DIFFICULTY	SERVES
10 minutes	5 minutes	● ○ ○	4

Most of the shrimp for sale in America is farmed in Asia, but the warm Gulf of Mexico waters are home to wild shrimp that are flavorful, tender, and sweet. Special shrimping boats catch them with nets. The lemon-butter sauce will have you reaching for seconds—and napkins! Don't forget a bowl for the shells!

INGREDIENTS
2 lemons
6 tablespoons butter
2 garlic cloves, minced
1 pound large shell-on
  shrimp (20 to 25)
2 tablespoons chopped
  fresh flat-leaf parsley
Crusty bread, for serving

1. Using a rasp-style grater, finely grate the zest from 1 lemon, then cut the lemon in half and squeeze out all the juice into a small bowl.

2. In a deep skillet, melt the butter, and then stir in the lemon zest, lemon juice, and garlic. Carefully add the shrimp and cook, stirring, just until the shrimp are pink on the outside and opaque throughout, about 5 minutes. (Opaque means they are no longer see-through, but a solid color; to avoid overcooking, don't wait until they're bright white.)

3. Transfer the shrimp with the sauce to a large bowl and sprinkle with parsley. Cut the remaining lemon into wedges, and serve with the shrimp and bread.

Eating in ALAS

If you think Alaska is a frozen tundra of polar bears and snow, you're in for a delicious surprise. So were the people who arrived from Asia 14,000 years ago. Ever since, their descendants have hunted moose, caribou, bear, whale, walrus, and seal, and fished for salmon and halibut. In summer, they still pick plants such as "beach asparagus," preserve highbush cranberries and crab apples, and dry fish and meat into long-lasting jerky to eat all winter.

Fishing and hunting are still very popular. Today, Alaskans put salmon in their sandwiches and moose on their spaghetti. People from across the country and around the world come here each summer to see the wildlife, and eat some of it, too.

Even the warmest days here don't involve shorts or swimming. But what makes summer amazing isn't the temperature—it's the sunshine! In June, parts of Alaska get 20 hours of light each day! All that sun can make garden vegetables grow to miraculous sizes. One cantaloupe grew to 65 pounds, while a record-breaking cabbage weighed 138 pounds—perfect for making coleslaw to serve with grizzly-bear burgers.

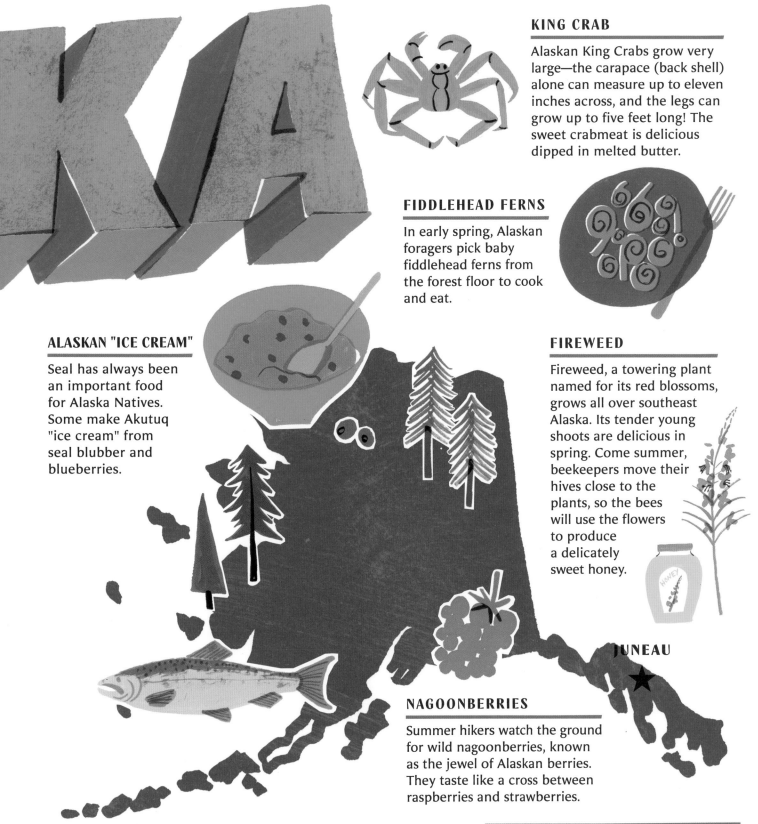

KING CRAB

Alaskan King Crabs grow very large—the carapace (back shell) alone can measure up to eleven inches across, and the legs can grow up to five feet long! The sweet crabmeat is delicious dipped in melted butter.

FIDDLEHEAD FERNS

In early spring, Alaskan foragers pick baby fiddlehead ferns from the forest floor to cook and eat.

ALASKAN "ICE CREAM"

Seal has always been an important food for Alaska Natives. Some make Akutuq "ice cream" from seal blubber and blueberries.

FIREWEED

Fireweed, a towering plant named for its red blossoms, grows all over southeast Alaska. Its tender young shoots are delicious in spring. Come summer, beekeepers move their hives close to the plants, so the bees will use the flowers to produce a delicately sweet honey.

JUNEAU

NAGOONBERRIES

Summer hikers watch the ground for wild nagoonberries, known as the jewel of Alaskan berries. They taste like a cross between raspberries and strawberries.

DEEP-FRIED PORK HOCK

Nearly ten percent of Alaskans are immigrants, while another nine percent were born to immigrant parents. Filipinos, the largest immigrant group in Alaska, have brought favorite dishes including deep-fried pork hock.

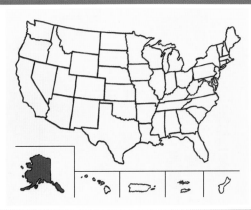

Smoked Salmon Cream Cheese Spread

PREPARATION TIME	LEVEL OF DIFFICULTY	MAKES
10 minutes	● ○ ○	about 2 cups

Grizzly bears aren't the only ones who enjoy wild Alaska salmon outdoors. This spread is perfect to pack into a cooler for a mountain hike or a glacial kayak trip. Be sure to use Alaskan smoked salmon, which is hot-smoked, rather than cold-smoked "lox."

INGREDIENTS

1 package (8 ounces) cream cheese, softened
½ cup sour cream
1 lemon
4 ounces hot-smoked salmon, skin removed and fish finely chopped
Coarse salt and freshly ground pepper (optional)
Chopped fresh flat-leaf parsley, for garnish
Crackers and sliced vegetables, for serving

1. In a bowl, blend together cream cheese and sour cream with a flexible spatula until smooth. Using a rasp-style grater, finely grate the zest of the lemon and then squeeze out all the juice into a small bowl. Add the zest and 1 tablespoon of the juice to the cream cheese mixture and stir until smooth.

2. Fold in the chopped salmon until it's well blended, then season with salt and pepper, if desired. Sprinkle the spread with parsley and serve with crackers and sliced vegetables. (The spread can be covered and refrigerated for up to 1 day.)

Eating in ARIZO

Some say this state takes its name from the phrase "arid zone," meaning dry area. And boy, is it *dry*! The Sonoran Desert covers parts of Arizona, where as little as four inches of rain fall in a whole year, and summer temperatures can top 120 degrees! Even so, people have called this place home for thousands of years and still find plenty of delicious things to eat growing right in the desert.

The native Tohono O'odham people dug irrigation canals to grow corn, but they found many other foods that grow wild in Arizona—without being watered at all. Mesquite trees produce bean pods that can be ground into a tasty flour. Tiny but super-spicy chiltepin peppers are used as a seasoning (and as medicine). And Arizonans long ago figured out how to eat different types of cactus! Barrel cactus fruit is ripe when it turns yellow. Cholla cactus buds taste like strawberries or kiwi fruit. And the prickly pear cactus can be eaten two ways: the broad green paddles, known as nopales, are popular in salads and tacos, and the sweet, pink-purple fruits make a delicious dessert, once you remove their sharp spines!

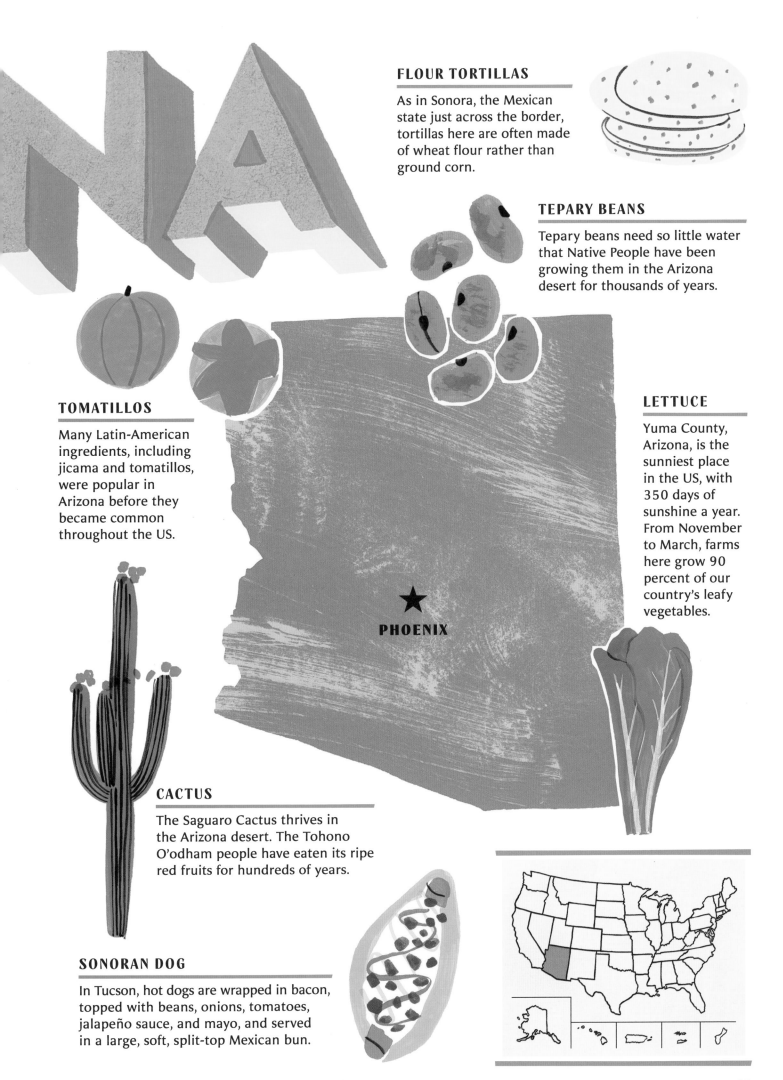

FLOUR TORTILLAS

As in Sonora, the Mexican state just across the border, tortillas here are often made of wheat flour rather than ground corn.

TEPARY BEANS

Tepary beans need so little water that Native People have been growing them in the Arizona desert for thousands of years.

TOMATILLOS

Many Latin-American ingredients, including jicama and tomatillos, were popular in Arizona before they became common throughout the US.

LETTUCE

Yuma County, Arizona, is the sunniest place in the US, with 350 days of sunshine a year. From November to March, farms here grow 90 percent of our country's leafy vegetables.

★
PHOENIX

CACTUS

The Saguaro Cactus thrives in the Arizona desert. The Tohono O'odham people have eaten its ripe red fruits for hundreds of years.

SONORAN DOG

In Tucson, hot dogs are wrapped in bacon, topped with beans, onions, tomatoes, jalapeño sauce, and mayo, and served in a large, soft, split-top Mexican bun.

Guacamole

PREPARATION TIME	LEVEL OF DIFFICULTY	SERVES
15 minutes	● ○ ○	4

People love to order guacamole in restaurants, but it's one of the easiest recipes to make at home! The only essential step is to start with perfectly ripe avocados: not too hard or too soft. They should feel heavy, and yield to gentle pressure around the stem. But don't squeeze too hard—save your strength for mashing the guac!

INGREDIENTS

3 tablespoons fresh lime juice (from 2 to 3 limes)
1 clove garlic, minced
¼ cup finely chopped red onion
1 small jalapeño pepper, seeded and finely chopped (optional)
3 ripe but firm avocados, peeled, pitted, and chopped
¼ cup chopped fresh cilantro
Coarse salt

1. In a bowl, combine the lime juice, garlic, and onion. Let rest for 5–10 minutes while you prepare the other ingredients. (The lime juice helps mellow the raw garlic and onion.)

2. Add in the jalapeño and avocado and mash with a fork to combine. Fold in the cilantro and salt to taste.

3. Serve immediately, or press plastic wrap onto the surface of the guacamole and refrigerate for up to 8 hours.

TIP: To peel and pit an avocado, first slice around the avocado from stem tip to bottom with a sharp knife. Then, gently pull apart the halves. Stick the sharp blade of the knife into the pit and pull it out with a slight twist. Use a large spoon to work your way around the avocado, between the peel and the fruit (yes, it's a fruit!), and scoop out the light green flesh. Now you are ready to slice, chop, or mash it.

Eating in ARKAN...

Known as the Natural State, Arkansas has remarkable natural resources, including gold and diamonds, as well as the foundations of good food: fertile soil, fresh water, and plentiful fish and game. All this natural abundance is reflected on dinner tables across the state. Many Arkansans go hunting and fishing, often feasting on trout, bass, squirrel, venison, and wild turkey alongside homegrown vegetables: tomatoes, cucumbers, summer squash, purple hull peas, turnip greens, okra, and rutabaga.

There are dozens of ways to prepare veggies but in Arkansas, the most popular way is fried to a crisp. Arkansas is especially famous for the fried dill pickle, invented in the town of Atkins in 1963 and served with ranch dressing for dipping. Head to the state fair in October to sample deep-fried corn on the cob and even fried watermelon! Whichever way you like your fruits and vegetables, be sure to wash them down with Arkansas's own spring water from the Ozark Mountains, another natural resource!

DUTCH OVEN

The Dutch oven is the state's official cooking vessel. Arkansans bury the ovens in coals to cook classic campfire meals.

WATERMELON

Some of the world's largest watermelons are grown in the city of Hope. One record-breaker weighed 268 pounds!

LITTLE ROCK

RICE

Arkansas farms grow the most rice of any state—and almost half the rice in America!

BISCUITS AND CHOCOLATE GRAVY

Southerners love biscuits and gravy for breakfast. In Arkansas, the gravy is sometimes made of chocolate!

SPINACH

The city of Alma is called the "Spinach Capital of the World." It puts about 60 million pounds of spinach into cans each year, and hosts an annual spinach festival.

Arkansas

Buttermilk Biscuits with Sawmill Gravy

PREPARATION TIME	COOKING TIME	LEVEL OF DIFFICULTY	SERVES
25 minutes (includes 10 minutes chilling time)	40 minutes	● ● ●	6

In this classic Southern breakfast, featherlight, piping-hot buttermilk biscuits are split in half and covered with a rich sausage sauce. The biscuits aren't just for breakfast—serve them at lunch or dinner next to chicken, or pile them with fruit and whipped cream for dessert!

INGREDIENTS

For the biscuits:
2½ cups all-purpose flour
½ teaspoon coarse salt
1 tablespoon baking powder
1 teaspoon baking soda
1 stick cold unsalted butter, cut into ½-inch cubes
1 cup cold buttermilk
2 tablespoons heavy (whipping) cream (optional)

For the gravy:
¾ pound loose pork breakfast sausage
¼ cup all-purpose flour
2½ cups milk
½ teaspoon freshly ground black pepper
¼ teaspoon cayenne pepper (optional)
Coarse salt

1. Make the biscuits: Preheat the oven to 450°F.

2. In a medium bowl, whisk to combine the flour, salt, baking powder, and baking soda. Using a pastry blender or your fingertips, quickly work the cubes of butter into the flour mixture (this is called "cutting it in") just until small clumps form. (You want the butter to be blended into the flour but not completely; the small clumps are what make the biscuits flaky.) Place the bowl in the refrigerator for 10 minutes to chill.

3. Add the cold buttermilk to the flour mixture and stir gently with a fork just until the dough comes together. (Be careful not to over mix, to keep the biscuits light instead of heavy.) Lightly flour a work surface, and then transfer the dough onto it. Gently knead 5 or 6 times, just until combined. Lightly flour your hands and press the dough into a rectangle about ¾ inch thick. Cut into 2-inch rounds with a biscuit cutter or small drinking glass and place on an ungreased baking sheet. Gently reshape the scraps and cut out more biscuits.

4. Brush the tops of the biscuits with cream, if using. Bake until biscuits are golden brown, 16–18 minutes, turning the baking sheet around in the oven halfway through. Transfer to a wire rack.

5. Make the gravy: While the biscuits are baking, cook the sausage in a large skillet over medium-high heat, breaking it up with a wooden spoon, until dark golden and crispy brown, 8–10 minutes.

6. Reduce the heat to medium, stir in the flour, and cook for 3 minutes. Stir in the milk, black pepper, and cayenne, if desired. Bring to a simmer and cook over medium-low heat, stirring occasionally, until thickened, 6–8 minutes. Season to taste with salt. Serve immediately over split biscuits.

Eating in CALIFO

The Golden State takes its nickname from the 1848 Gold Rush, when people poured in with hopes of striking it rich. Over time, others came pursuing different dreams, and they've never stopped. It's now the most populated state in America.

Some people came to California for the rich farmland, some came to work on the railroads; others for the movie industry in Hollywood, or more recently, Silicon Valley. Immigrants have brought recipes from around the world. Californians were among the first Americans to taste tacos, sushi, and smoothies. Local chefs began combining food from around the world into delicious new dishes, like putting Korean kimchi on top of Mexican tacos—yum! Many of these tasty mash-ups then made their way all over the country.

California is home to more than one American Dream. It offered the dream of convenience cooking—canned vegetables, drive-in restaurants, and fast food. Up in the Bay Area, people dreamed of a different kind of eating, with the freshest ingredients directly from the state's famous farms. But no matter where in America you live, if you eat artichokes, almonds, avocados, raisins, or walnuts, chances are, they were grown in California.

RNIA

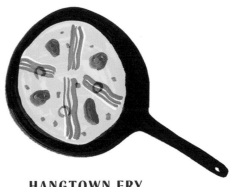

HANGTOWN FRY

Hangtown fry—a luxurious dish of eggs, oysters, and bacon—was invented during the Gold Rush, as a breakfast for miners who struck gold and became rich.

FORTUNE COOKIES

Asian immigrants brought sushi, ramen, pho, and dumplings. Fortune cookies became popular in San Fransisco's Chinatown, and Sriracha hot sauce has been made in Los Angeles since 1980.

YOU WILL LEAD A LUCKY LIFE

SACRAMENTO

CIOPPINO

San Francisco is called "the City by the Bay," and that bay feeds locals very well. Cioppino, the city's famous fishermen's stew, is chock-full of shrimp, scallops, crab, and clams.

FISH TACOS

California doesn't just border Mexico— it was part of that country until 1848. Today, people still feast on Mexican food here, from fish tacos in Baja to Mission-style burritos in the Bay Area.

FRESH PRODUCE

The farms in California's 500-mile-long Central Valley grow everything from almonds to artichokes. This valley produces more than half of America's fruits, vegetables, and nuts.

FARMERS' MARKETS

California sparked America's farmers' market obsession. At San Francisco's Ferry Plaza, dozens of farmers sell spectacular local fruits, vegetables, fish, cheese, and more.

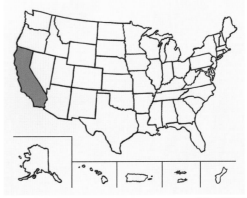

Cobb Salad

PREPARATION TIME	LEVEL OF DIFFICULTY	SERVES
30 minutes	● ○ ○	6

California could be called "The Salad State." Caesar salad, Cobb salad, Green Goddess dressing, and mesclun greens all took root here, and are now salad-bowl staples across America and beyond. This one, named for owner Robert Cobb of Hollywood's Brown Derby restaurant, is a great way to turn leftovers into a fresh, protein-packed dinner. If you have extra cooked chicken, bacon, or hard-boiled eggs in the fridge, just add fresh greens and crumbled blue cheese. It's traditional to arrange each ingredient in a row over the bed of lettuce, like an edible work of art!

INGREDIENTS
1 large head romaine
    lettuce, finely chopped
6 slices bacon, cooked and
    coarsely chopped
2 chicken breasts, cooked
    and sliced
2 tomatoes, cut into wedges
2 hard-boiled eggs, peeled
    and cut into four pieces
2 ripe but firm avocados,
    peeled, pitted, and
    coarsely chopped
½ cup finely crumbled blue
    cheese
¼ cup red wine vinegar
½ cup extra-virgin olive oil
1 tablespoon Dijon mustard
Salt and freshly ground
    black pepper

1. Spread the lettuce in an even layer on a large serving platter.

2. Arrange the bacon, chicken, tomatoes, eggs, avocado, and blue cheese in neat rows on top of the lettuce.

3. In a small bowl, whisk together the vinegar, oil, and mustard until well combined, then season to taste with salt and pepper.

4. Drizzle over the salad and serve.

TIP: To make hard-boiled eggs, first set up a bowl of ice and water. Place eggs in a pot and cover with cold water. Bring to a boil over medium-high heat. Immediately remove from the heat, cover, and let sit for 8 minutes. Using a slotted spoon, transfer eggs to the ice water and let sit for a few minutes before peeling.

Eating in COLORADO

Colorado didn't become a state until 100 years after America became a country—that's why it's known as the Centennial State. Geography here varies from the towering Rocky Mountains to flat-as-pancakes prairies. The first Spanish explorers named its largest river *Rio Colorado* because it is "colored red." (Their chili is red, too!) That famous red river is still mighty today, and many people go fishing in it for largemouth bass and rainbow trout. Bison and cattle roam the far-ranging plains, and while many of the state's Old West towns have been replaced by modern big cities, the original rugged spirit is alive and well, as are appetites for hearty cowboy cooking.

Meanwhile, clear "bluebird" skies (meaning there's not a cloud to be seen) with bountiful sunshine nourish many plants. Farmed favorites include sweet Palisade peaches and spicy pueblo chiles, a key ingredient in one local specialty, the chile-and-cheese-smothered "slopper" burger. Coloradans also forage for wild foods, including strawberries and mushrooms. The state's natural beauty provides so much fresh food and so many opportunities for outdoor adventure (like skiing and hiking) that its residents are some of the healthiest people in the United States.

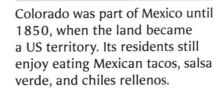

MEXICAN FOOD

Colorado was part of Mexico until 1850, when the land became a US territory. Its residents still enjoy eating Mexican tacos, salsa verde, and chiles rellenos.

RATTLESNAKE

Thirty minutes west of Denver, in an "Old West" restaurant called The Fort, you can eat rattlesnake cakes, elk chops, and bison tongue.

LAMB

This state's dry pastureland is perfect for raising sheep, so chefs across the country cook Colorado lamb.

CANTALOUPE

The town of Rocky Ford has been famous for its sweet cantaloupe since the 1880s.

★
DENVER

CORN

The town of Olathe is famous for its sweet corn. The crop is so tender and sweet that it's shipped all over the country. Thousands of people attend the town's corn festival each August.

POTATOES

Much of Colorado is a mile or more above sea level. You can avoid altitude sickness by eating foods high in potassium, like watermelon and potatoes.

ROCKY MOUNTAIN OYSTERS

Landlocked Colorado has a special "oyster" that's not a shellfish at all. Beef testicles are breaded and deep-fried to make Rocky Mountain oysters.

ROCKY MOUNTAIN OYSTERS

Cowboy Charro Beans

PREPARATION TIME	COOKING TIME	LEVEL OF DIFFICULTY	SERVES
15 minutes, plus overnight soaking time	3 hours	● ● ○	4-6

Cowboys have always loved a delicious pot of beans, often cooked right over a campfire after a long day in the saddle. This stovetop version is a little soupy and deliciously porky. Try it over rice or with warm tortillas.

INGREDIENTS

1 pound dried pinto beans, rinsed

¾ pound thick-cut bacon, cut crosswise into ¼ inch pieces

1 large yellow onion, coarsely chopped

1 head garlic (about 10 cloves), cloves separated, smashed and peeled

1–2 jalapeño peppers, cut in half lengthwise and ribs and seeds removed (optional)

3–4 sprigs fresh thyme

2 sprigs fresh oregano

2 bay leaves

Coarse salt and freshly ground black pepper

1. Place the beans in a bowl with water to cover by several inches and let soak overnight. Drain well. (Or, if you're in a hurry, try this shortcut: Bring beans and enough water to cover by an inch to a boil in a large pot; turn off the heat, and let it stand, covered, for 1 hour. Drain beans well.)

2. Heat a Dutch oven or other large heavy pot over medium. Add the bacon and cook, stirring, until it begins to release its fat and starts to brown, about 5 minutes. Add the onion and cook, stirring, until tender and golden brown, 5–7 minutes.

3. Add 7 cups water, the soaked beans, garlic, jalapeños (if using), thyme, oregano, bay leaves, and 1 teaspoon salt. Bring to a boil over high heat, then reduce to a simmer and cook until the beans are very tender, 2–3 hours. Season to taste with salt and pepper. Remove the bay leaves, herb sprigs, and jalapeños, and serve.

Eating in CONNECT

Residents of Connecticut are famous for their ingenuity and innovation, claiming such inventions as the cotton gin, the sewing machine, the typewriter, the can opener, and the Frisbee. Some historians say the state was the home of the first written constitution (way back in the 1630s), hence its nickname, the Constitution State. This can-do spirit shines in the state's foods as well.

Connecticut is the birthplace of the first lobster roll, and today they're still served all over the state. (And unlike in other states, they're served hot!) Some locals claim the hamburger is a Connecticut invention, although others disagree. And residents of Hartford, the state capital, make their own dessert, too: Election Cake, a nutmeg-spiced baked treat traditionally served when voters go to the polls. What will these clever Connecticuters think up next?

STEAMED HAMBURGER

While most hamburger patties are fried or grilled, some diners in Connecticut steam them instead. They're juicy, not dry.

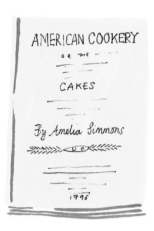

AMERICAN COOKERY

The first American cookbook was published in Hartford in 1796. Until then, Americans used British cookbooks. Amelia Simmons's *American Cookery* printed the first written recipes for corn cakes, broiled shad, roast turkey, cranberry sauce, and pumpkin pie!

PICKLE

In Connecticut, a law requires that a pickle has to bounce to be classified as a pickle.

★
HARTFORD

NUTMEGS

Connecticut is also nicknamed the Nutmeg State. Legend has it that early Connecticut residents would shape fake spices from wood and sell them as authentic.

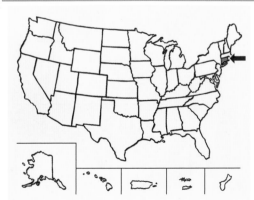

WILD SHAD

Wild shad fish swim from the open ocean up through Connecticut's rivers each spring. They were a staple food for Native Americans and are now the state's official fish. The town of Essex holds a giant outdoor shad bake each June.

Clam Pizza

PREPARATION TIME	COOKING TIME	LEVEL OF DIFFICULTY	SERVES
30 minutes, plus dough rising time	10 minutes	● ● ●	4

The coastal city of New Haven claims to be the birthplace of clam pizza, a regional recipe that is unusual for the toppings it has (littleneck clams) and those that it *doesn't have* (tomato sauce and mozzarella). If you don't love clams, you can top the thin Neapolitan-style crust with anything you like, but these mollusks are mighty delicious.

INGREDIENTS

3½ cups all-purpose flour

1½ teaspoons active dry yeast

2 teaspoons salt

2 teaspoons sugar

¼ cup plus 2 tablespoons extra-virgin olive oil

2 dozen littleneck (hard shell) clams, scrubbed and shucked, cut into bite-sized pieces if large

2 cloves garlic, peeled and thinly sliced

Coarse salt and freshly ground black pepper or crushed chili flakes (optional)

2 tablespoons chopped fresh parsley

SPECIAL EQUIPMENT

(optional): pizza stone, pizza peel

1. Preheat the oven to 500°F. If you have a pizza stone, preheat it in the oven.

2. In a large bowl, whisk together the flour, yeast, salt, and sugar. Make a well in the center and add 3 tablespoons of the olive oil and 1 cup lukewarm water (this means it's just a little warmer than your own body temperature; try running water over your wrist to test it). Stir well. If necessary, add a little more water to make a workable but sticky dough. Lightly flour a work surface, and turn out dough onto it. Knead for a few minutes. Place 1 tablespoon of the oil in a clean bowl. Add the dough and turn to coat it with oil. Cover with a damp kitchen towel and let rise until doubled in bulk, about 1 hour. (The dough can be made ahead of time, before rising, and refrigerated for up to 24 hours. When ready to use, remove the dough from the refrigerator, punch down, and bring to room temperature before rolling and baking.)

3. On a pizza peel, roll the dough to a large, ¼-inch-thick round. (If you don't have a pizza peel or stone, roll the dough on a floured surface and slide it onto a baking sheet, reshaping it if necessary.) Allow the dough to rest for 10 minutes. Punch it down and stretch it slightly. Brush the remaining 2 tablespoons olive oil over the top of the dough. Sprinkle the clams and garlic over the top and season to taste with salt and pepper or chili flakes, if using.

4. Slide the pizza onto the hot stone with the pizza peel (or put the baking sheet in the oven). Bake until golden brown, about 10 minutes (a few minutes longer if using a baking sheet). Remove pizza from oven (using the pizza peel if the pizza is on a stone), sprinkle evenly with parsley, and serve immediately.

Tip: Work with an adult to shuck clams (or ask a fishmonger to do this for you). First, scrub the shells with a firm brush to remove any grit. Wearing work gloves, hold clams one by one, flat side up, and wedge a small knife between the halves. Twist, and then pry apart the shells.

Eating in DELAW

Delaware is a small state, but it's got a big draw: beautiful beaches. Those sandy coastlines make it a vacation destination.

All summer, families crowd into shore towns such as Rehoboth Beach for sand, surf, carnival rides, cotton candy, saltwater taffy, caramel popcorn, and French fries sprinkled with vinegar. But the best beach food is the ocean-caught seafood. Vacationers eat fresh oysters, spiced shrimp, blue crabs, pasta tossed with scallops and shrimp, or rockfish, which is itself sometimes served stuffed with even more crab and shrimp! Crab-house restaurants spread newspapers on outdoor tables where families order crab soup and crab cakes, and use little hammers to crack piles of boiled crabs.

Further inland on the Delmarva Peninsula (so named because it's where Delaware, Maryland, and Virginia meet), Sussex County is home to the busiest chicken farms in America. Residents cook roast chicken, chicken and dumplings, or beach-ready chicken salad sandwiches. All summer, roadside stands sell barbecued chicken, which vacationers buy while driving to and from the beach.

Don't forget the ice cream! Delaware is home to many dairy farms and is dotted with plenty of parlors. Get a big cone topped with Delaware's favorite flavor: peach.

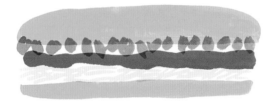

THE BOBBIE

Delaware's signature sandwich is the Bobbie. It includes the best flavors of Thanksgiving—roast turkey, cranberry sauce, and stuffing—served together on a roll, any day of the year.

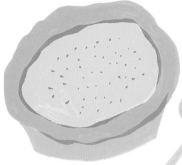

POTATO PIE

An old Delaware recipe for potato pie features white spuds—not sweet potatoes!

CHICKEN

One of Delaware's nicknames is the Blue Hen State, for the chickens that accompanied the state's soldiers in the American Revolution. Today, poultry farming is so big here that chickens outnumber people by more than 200 to 1!

DOVER

LIMA BEANS

Farmers in Delaware grow more lima beans than in any other state. The tender, sweet beans go into succotash and chicken soup, or are simply simmered and tossed with butter.

SLIPPERY DUMPLINGS

"Slippery dumplings" are a state favorite. The delicious squares of dough are more like pasta than biscuits, and they definitely live up to their name.

MUSKRAT

The furry muskrat is prized for its pelt, and some people here eat it, too, either stewed or grilled.

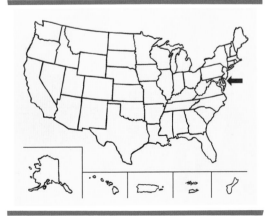

PEACH PIE

Peach pie is the official dessert of Delaware, where peaches have grown for hundreds of years.

Strawberry Shortcake

PREPARATION TIME	COOKING TIME	LEVEL OF DIFFICULTY	SERVES
50 minutes	15 minutes	● ● ○	6

This springtime dessert, a classic from coast to coast, has special significance in Delaware, where strawberries are the official state fruit. Delaware celebrates strawberry week each May, when the little berries are ripe for the picking, and many families load up on the sweet harvest at "pick your own" farms.

INGREDIENTS

For the strawberries:

2 pints strawberries, green tops removed and fruit cut in half (or in quarters if large)

2 tablespoons sugar, or more to taste

For the shortcakes:

2 cups all-purpose flour, plus more for work surface

2 tablespoons sugar

1 tablespoon plus 1 teaspoon baking powder

1 teaspoon salt

4 tablespoons cold unsalted butter, cut into ½-inch cubes

2½ cups heavy (whipping) cream

½ teaspoon pure vanilla extract

SPECIAL EQUIPMENT

3-inch round cutter (or a drinking glass with rim about that size)

1. Prepare the strawberries: In a bowl, toss the strawberries with sugar. Cover and set aside at room temperature for 30 minutes or up to several hours. (The berries will release juice and become more flavorful as they sit.)

2. Position a rack in the middle of the oven and preheat to 425°F. Line a baking sheet with parchment paper.

3. Meanwhile, make the shortcakes: In a medium bowl, whisk to combine the flour, sugar, baking powder, and salt. Using a pastry blender or your fingertips, quickly work the cubes of butter into the flour mixture just until small clumps form. (You want the butter to be blended into the flour but not completely; the small clumps are what make the shortcakes flaky.) Add 1 cup of the cream and stir gently with a fork just until the dough comes together. (Be careful not to over mix, to keep the biscuits light instead of heavy.)

4. Lightly flour a work surface, and then turn the dough out onto it. With a rolling pin, roll the dough until it's about 2 inches thick. Using the cutter or drinking glass rim, cut the dough into rounds and place on the baking sheet. Gently reshape the scraps and cut out more biscuits.

5. Bake until light golden around the edges, 10–12 minutes, rotating sheet halfway through (this means turning it front to back on the oven rack, for even baking). Transfer shortcakes to a wire rack. While the shortcakes are still warm, split them in half horizontally.

6. In a bowl, with an electric mixer, beat the remaining 1½ cups cream with the vanilla just until soft peaks form (do not over mix). Serve the split shortcakes with generous scoops of berries and whipped cream in the middle.

Eating in FLORIDA

It's always sunny in the Sunshine State. Many children who live in Florida have never seen snow. All this tropical weather allows farmers to grow all kinds of fruit, including lots of citrus. For most of the year, 90 percent of America's orange juice comes from Florida farms. Lemons, limes, tangerines, and grapefruit grow just as well in the Florida sun, as do other tropical fruits, like pineapple, mango, and guava. There's also sugarcane, and the jamfruit tree, whose cherry-like fruit is as sweet as cotton candy!

Warmwater beaches surround Florida on three sides. Fish such as grouper, pompano, and mullet are all delicious for dinner, especially with a squeeze of locally grown citrus.

Florida also feels tropical because many residents emigrated from nearby islands including Cuba, Jamaica, Haiti, and the Bahamas, and the food on Florida tables reflects those flavors. In Miami, you can enjoy Caribbean dishes such as mashed yucca (a starchy vegetable also used to make tapioca), fried plantains (they look like big bananas), and *arroz con pollo* (chicken and rice, often with bell peppers and olives). And for dessert, it's Key lime pie, made with fresh little limes that grow on the sunny islands called the Florida Keys.

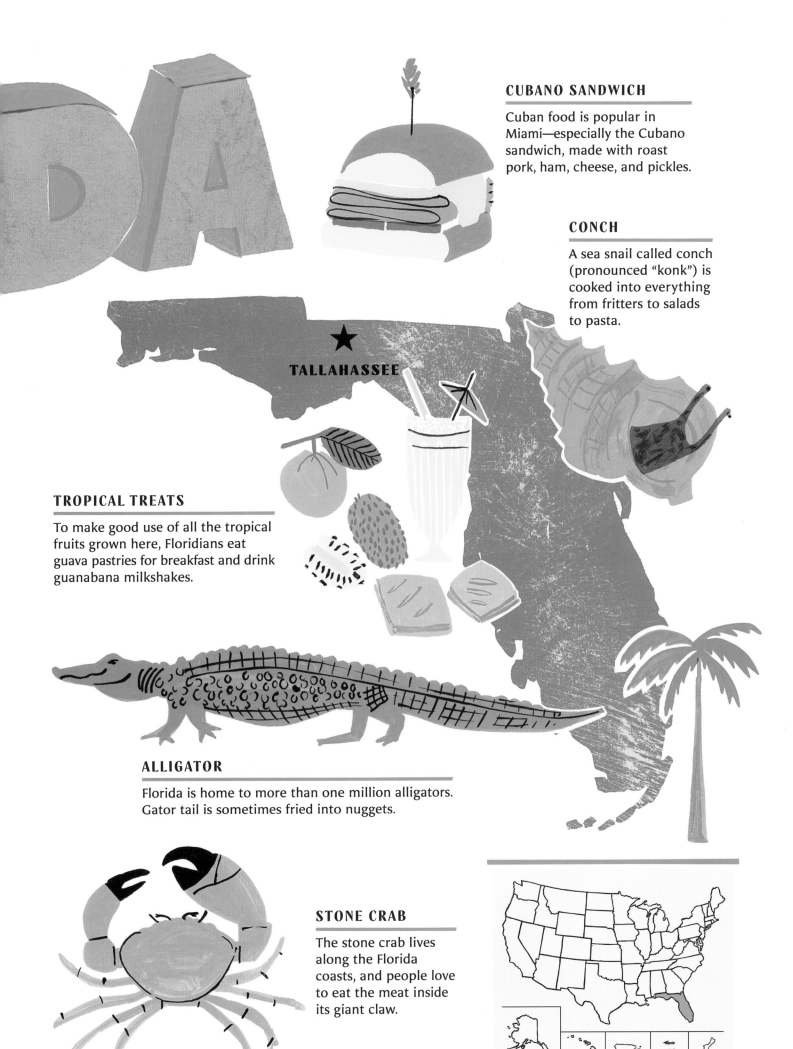

CUBANO SANDWICH

Cuban food is popular in Miami—especially the Cubano sandwich, made with roast pork, ham, cheese, and pickles.

CONCH

A sea snail called conch (pronounced "konk") is cooked into everything from fritters to salads to pasta.

TROPICAL TREATS

To make good use of all the tropical fruits grown here, Floridians eat guava pastries for breakfast and drink guanabana milkshakes.

TALLAHASSEE

ALLIGATOR

Florida is home to more than one million alligators. Gator tail is sometimes fried into nuggets.

STONE CRAB

The stone crab lives along the Florida coasts, and people love to eat the meat inside its giant claw.

Key Lime Pie

PREPARATION TIME	COOKING TIME	LEVEL OF DIFFICULTY	SERVES
5 hours (includes 4 hours chilling time)	25 minutes	● ○ ○	8–10

Key limes are yellowish green (rather than bright green), with a thin skin and a slightly tarter flavor than the more common Persian limes. They are usually sold in net bags; look for them at large supermarkets or specialty grocers.

INGREDIENTS

For the crust:
12 standard graham crackers (about 6½ ounces), broken into pieces
2 tablespoons sugar
6 tablespoons unsalted butter, melted
Pinch of coarse salt

For the filling:
1 (14-ounce) can sweetened condensed milk
4 large egg yolks
½ cup lime juice, preferably from fresh Key limes

For the topping:
1 cup heavy (whipping) cream
1 tablespoon powdered sugar

SPECIAL EQUIPMENT
food processor, 9-inch pie plate

1. Preheat the oven to 350°F.

2. Make the crust: In a food processor, pulse the graham crackers until coarse crumbs form (you should have about 1½ cups). Add the sugar and pulse until crumbs are fine. Add the melted butter and pinch of salt and process until incorporated and the crumbs look like wet sand.

3. Turn the crumbs out into the pie plate and use the bottom of a measuring cup to press the crumbs evenly over the bottom and the sides of the plate. Bake until the crust is fragrant, about 10 minutes, then transfer pie plate to a wire rack and let crust cool completely.

4. Make the filling: In a large bowl, whisk together the condensed milk and egg yolks until completely smooth, with no streaks remaining. Whisk in the lime juice. Pour the filling into the cooled crust and bake until barely set, about 15 minutes.

5. Transfer to a wire rack and let cool completely. Refrigerate pie until well chilled, at least 4 hours and up to 3 days, covered.

6. Make the topping: In a bowl, with an electric mixer, beat the cream with the sugar just until soft peaks form (do not over mix). Serve pie with whipped cream.

Tip: If you don't have a food processor, put the crackers in a resealable plastic bag and use a rolling pin to crush them into crumbs. Then, transfer the crumbs to a bowl and stir in the sugar and butter.

Eating in GEOR

Atlanta is Georgia's capital, and the unofficial capital of the South. It has a strong African-American community, rich in tradition and history. Today, it's an international city, where nearly one in ten residents are immigrants. Atlanta's food reflects this—you'll find trendy restaurant dishes like heirloom grits with pastured pork, excellent Mexican tacos and tamales, Caribbean jerk chicken and fried plantains, and, from across Africa, *jollof* rice and *boerewors* sausage.

That's the New South. But in Georgia, you can find the *Old* South, too. That means city tearooms with old recipes and rural mansions that were once plantations. You'll find gracious Southern hospitality, complete with heaping helpings of Dixie favorites: fried chicken, baked ham, butter beans, fried okra, fried green tomatoes, Savannah red rice, and collard greens, salty from the hambone they were braised with.

Farmers' markets overflow with Southern bounty, including the crops that earn Georgia the nicknames "The Peach State" and "The Goober State" (Goober means peanuts in the Bantu family of African languages). Both crops find their way into plenty of desserts, but save room for caramel cake, banana pudding, or a slice of coconut cream pie, too.

WILD PIG

For more than 50 years, Georgia politicians have served wild pigs at an annual feast to mark the start of their legislative session.

NUTS

Georgia is nuts about nuts! It's America's pecan capital and grows almost half of the country's peanut crop. A peanut farmer named Jimmy Carter, from the city of Americus, became the 39th US president.

ATLANTA

VIDALIA ONION

Georgia's Vidalia onions are so mild and sweet, some people eat them like apples.

PEACHES

Monks planted Georgia's first peach trees in the late 1500s. Today, the state's orchards send the fruit around the world.

HONEY

When the Tupelo trees bloom in April or May, visiting bees make a delicate honey with a flavor so special, people have written songs about it.

COCA-COLA

Atlanta is home to the Coca-Cola Company's headquarters. Georgians often use the soda as an ingredient in recipes for glazed ham or cake.

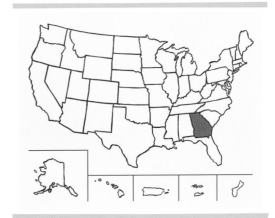

Peach and Vidalia Onion Salad

PREPARATION TIME	LEVEL OF DIFFICULTY	SERVES
15 minutes	● ○ ○	4

Two of Georgia's best-known harvests—peaches and Vidalia onions—meet in one delicious salad. You'll usually find peaches in desserts, like cobbler and pie, but they're just as tasty in savory dishes. This simple sweet-tart dish is wonderful with grilled chicken or pork, or next to a sandwich when it's too hot to cook!

INGREDIENTS
6 ripe but firm medium peaches
1 tablespoon fresh lemon juice
1 tablespoon honey
¼ cup thinly sliced Vidalia onion
16 large mint leaves
Coarse salt

1. Slice the peaches into wedges and toss with the lemon juice, honey, and Vidalia onion and season lightly with salt. Transfer to a serving platter.

2. Tear the mint leaves, sprinkle them over the salad, and serve.

Eating in GUAM

Guam became a US territory in 1950. Because of its geography and history, the tiny island boasts big flavors!

Six thousand miles west of California—out between Japan and Australia—this US territory has a coastal reef that for 4,000 years has been a prized source for foods such as fish, octopus, and seaweed. But Guamanians don't only eat from the ocean. The native Chamorro people have long feasted on delicious plants that include breadfruit, bananas, and root vegetables including cassava. Polynesian explorers brought coconut, known as "The Tree of Life," to the island. Dried coconut, coconut oil, and coconut water are used in many Guamanian recipes.

Guam was a colony of Spain for more than 200 years, and was occupied by Japan during World War Two. Today, Guam's food reflects flavors from many nations, especially its Pacific neighbors. You can eat Korean barbecue and Japanese-style sushi. One-third of the island's residents are from the Philippines, so Filipino favorites, like whole roast pig, are particularly popular. No matter the table where you gather on Guam, you can always ask for someone to pass the *finadene*, a condiment made with soy sauce, hot peppers, tomatoes, and onions. That blend of local ingredients and world cultures is the true taste of Guam.

BUNELOS AGA

Guamanians love a Chamorro treat called *bunelos aga*, donut balls made of deep-fried mashed banana!

ESCABECHE

When the Spanish colonized Guam, they brought many of their national dishes. Today, islanders still use a Spanish recipe for fish cooked in vinegar sauce called *escabeche*.

LUMPIA

Guamanians adopted many delicious dishes from their Filipino neighbors, like *lumpia* rolls filled with ground pork or beef.

HAGANA

BREADFRUIT

Polynesian explorers brought breadfruit tree shoots to Guam, where the starchy fruit is now a local staple. It tastes like a cross between bread and sweet potatoes.

COCONUTS

The native Chamorro people have been using every part of the coconut tree for thousands of years. The dried coconut meat, called *copra*, became an important source of wealth in the 20th century.

Chicken Salad with Coconut

PREPARATION TIME	LEVEL OF DIFFICULTY	SERVES
20 minutes	● ● ○	4

This Guamanian version of chicken salad has wonderfully refreshing flavor, thanks to lots of lemon and fresh coconut. Fresh coconuts and frozen pieces are commonly found in Asian markets and many large supermarkets. Have an adult help you crack open a fresh one.

INGREDIENTS
3–4 lemons

1 rotisserie chicken (about 2 pounds), cooked

½ cup shredded frozen coconut (unsweetened) or 1 coconut, freshly grated

1 bunch scallions (about 5), roots trimmed, white and green parts thinly sliced

½ small red onion, finely chopped

2 jalapeño peppers, seeded and finely chopped (optional)

Coarse salt and freshly ground black pepper

1. With a rasp-style grater, finely zest 1 lemon. Cut all the lemons in half and squeeze over a liquid measuring cup until you get ½ cup juice.

2. Remove the skin from the chicken. Separate the meat from the bones, pull it into shreds, and transfer to a large bowl (you should have about 4 cups); discard bones. Add the lemon zest and juice, coconut, scallions, red onion, and jalapeños, if using, and toss well to combine.

3. Season the salad with salt and pepper, and serve.

Eating in HAWAII

Hawaii is an island paradise, complete with tropical beaches, hula dancers in grass skirts, and necklaces called *leis* made of fragrant flowers. The state's geography makes it unlike any other—and its food is unique, too! Hawaii is the only US state that is not part of North America: it is made up of eight islands in a part of the Pacific Ocean known as Oceania. It's more than 2,000 miles west of California, almost halfway to Australia! Did you know that before Hawaii became America's 50th state in 1959, it was an independent nation ruled by kings and queens?

The first people to arrive in Hawaii were Polynesians, who came by boat across the Pacific. Over time, settlers brought plants that flourished in the islands' rich volcanic soils, including coffee beans, macadamia nuts, sugarcane, and pineapples. Those crops eventually became main ingredients in Hawaiian cuisine. Today, if you visit Hawaii, you might enjoy fish fresh from the Pacific, such as ahi or aku tuna, or mahi mahi. You might also attend a luau, a giant outdoor banquet featuring roasted pork, mashed taro root, and plenty of coconuts and pineapples, all representing the delicious bounty of this tropical paradise.

SPAM

Hawaiians eat about six million cans of SPAM every year. That's an average of about 5 cans per person!

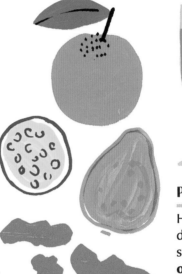

KALUA PIG

At *luau* celebrations, Hawaiians cook Kalua pig for 10 hours in an underground oven called an imu.

SHAVE ICE

Locals cool down with "shave ice," drenched in syrup with flavors including pineapple, pickled mango, and green tea. President Obama grew up here and orders shave ice when he comes back to visit.

HONOLULU ★

POG JUICE

Hawaiian children drink juice called POG, short for **p**assion fruit, **o**range, and **g**uava, all grown on the islands.

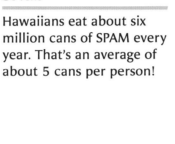

COFFEE BEANS

Hawaiian farmers have grown coffee for nearly 200 years. Today, they are famous for the crop, harvesting millions of pounds of coffee beans each year.

BOWL OF POI

Polynesian settlers who sailed across the Pacific brought taro, the base of a sticky, starchy pudding called poi.

Tofu Poké Bowl

PREPARATION TIME	COOKING TIME	LEVEL OF DIFFICULTY	SERVES
10 minutes, plus 30 minutes chilling time	30 minutes	● ● ○	4

Named for the Hawaiian word for "slice" or "cut" and pronounced "poh-KAY," a rice bowl like this would most often include chunks of tuna—or other super-fresh Pacific fish—marinated in sesame oil and soy sauce and eaten with chopsticks. In this vegetarian version, the rice is topped with marinated tofu instead of raw fish.

INGREDIENTS

1 (14-ounce) package firm tofu, drained
3 scallions, trimmed and very thinly sliced on the diagonal
¼ cup low-sodium soy sauce, plus more for serving
2 tablespoons toasted sesame oil
1 tablespoon toasted sesame seeds
2 teaspoons very finely chopped roasted macadamia nuts (optional)
Crushed chili flakes (optional), to taste
1½ cups short-grain white rice
Sliced avocado and radishes, for serving

1. Cut the tofu into 1-inch cubes and transfer to a large bowl. Add the scallions, soy sauce, sesame oil, sesame seeds, and macadamia nuts, if using, and gently toss to combine. Add crushed chili flakes, if desired. Refrigerate for about 30 minutes.

2. Meanwhile, rinse the rice in a sieve until the water runs clear. Combine the rice and 1½ cups water in a medium saucepan and bring to a boil. Reduce heat to low, cover, and cook until rice is tender, 18–22 minutes. Turn off the heat and let stand, covered, 10 minutes, and then fluff with a fork and keep warm.

3. Divide rice evenly into 4 serving bowls, and top with the tofu. Serve with avocado, radishes, and soy sauce.

Eating in IDAHO

On average, each American eats more than one hundred pounds of potatoes each year. Many of those potatoes come from Idaho, where farmers grow more of the crop than any other state! The big, starchy spuds that Americans enjoy baked to a fluff or fried to a crisp are called russet potatoes. Russets grow so well in this state's rich volcanic soil that many people across the country simply call them Idaho potatoes.

Idaho takes its name from a Shoshone word that means "gem of the mountains" and is known today as the Gem State. Come visit in summer and you might think the name came from the abundant wild huckleberries—they sparkle like purple jewels! Idahoans pick these berries and cook them in breakfast dishes and desserts.

In the 1800s, many Chinese immigrants moved to Idaho to work as gold miners. At one point, they made up a quarter of the state's population. The Chinese people planted some of the first gardens in the new towns. They also opened restaurants and grocery stores, introducing rice, noodles, and dumplings to the area. Today, Chinese restaurants are still popular across Idaho!

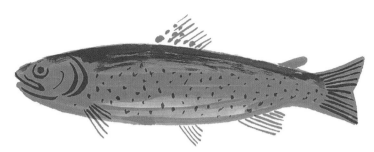

FINGER STEAKS

Crunchy, hot finger steaks are tiny strips of beef that are battered and fried. Idahoans enjoy them by the basketful!

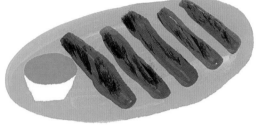

STEELHEAD TROUT

Every fall, people from all over travel to Idaho to fish for steelhead, a giant rainbow trout!

PURPLE FLOWERING CAMAS

The local Nez Perce tribe introduced hungry explorers Lewis and Clark to the purple camas, whose nutritious root tastes like pumpkin. They ate so much they got stomachaches!

HUCKLEBERRIES

Huckleberries are the state fruit of Idaho. Stop by any cafe and you'll likely find huckleberry pie, ice cream, or cookies on the menu.

BOISE

★

POTATOES

Idaho grows more than 10 billion pounds of potatoes per year. Spudnuts are a type of donut made from mashed potatoes.

PRONGHORN ANTELOPE

Pronghorn antelope are popular game for Idaho bow hunters. The meat can be cooked in stews, burgers, or breaded cutlets.

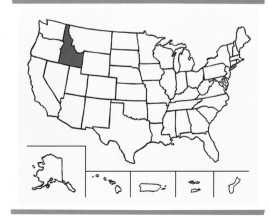

Twice-Baked Potatoes

PREPARATION TIME	COOKING TIME	LEVEL OF DIFFICULTY	SERVES
20 minutes	15 minutes	● ● ○	8

Think of this as the spud so nice, you bake it twice! Although served in their jackets, these have all the creamy richness of mashed potatoes. This recipe is also a great way to dress up leftover baked potatoes; just skip step 2 below.

INGREDIENTS
4 large russet (baking) potatoes (about 2 pounds)
1 tablespoon olive oil
½ teaspoon salt, plus more to taste
4 tablespoons unsalted butter
¼ cup sour cream
1 tablespoon milk
1 cup shredded cheddar cheese
2 tablespoons finely chopped fresh chives
Freshly ground black pepper

1. Preheat the oven to 425°F.

2. Scrub the potatoes well. Using a fork, prick each potato 3 or 4 times. Place on a baking sheet, brush with the olive oil, and sprinkle evenly with the ½ teaspoon salt. Bake until a paring knife can be easily inserted into and removed from the potato, 40–50 minutes. Transfer the potatoes to a plate to cool but leave the oven on.

3. When the potatoes are cool enough to handle, halve them lengthwise. Scrape the flesh of the potato into a bowl, leaving ⅛ inch of potato on the skin. Add the butter, sour cream, milk, ½ cup of cheddar, the chives, and salt and pepper to taste. With a potato masher or a fork, mash the mixture until smooth.

4. Divide the potato mixture evenly among the skins. Top with the remaining ½ cup cheddar. Return to oven and bake until the potatoes are heated through and the cheddar is melted, 20–25 minutes. Serve immediately.

Eating in ILLINO

Back when most Americans had farms, they raised their own meat. People in cities bought meat in butcher shops, until a century ago, when Illinois changed all that. With the rise of railroads and refrigeration, farms across the Midwest sent their cattle, pigs, and sheep to Chicago's giant stockyards. The Union Stock Yards were the world's largest meatpacking district, processing millions of animals a year. Thousands of workers butchered day and night, supplying pre-cut, plastic-wrapped beef and pork to grocery stores from coast to coast. The city of Chicago had to change the direction of the river that flowed through the stockyards to keep the city drinking water safe!

The Union Stock Yards are gone now, but meat is still on the menu. German and Polish immigrants made hams and sausage into serious business in Illinois. Hot dogs, sold at the 1893 World's Fair in Chicago, are still everyone's favorite snack at a Cubs or White Sox game. When you visit, save room for Chicago's signature street food, a juicy Italian beef sandwich. Or, splurge on a prime rib steak in one of the city's famous steakhouses!

DEEP-DISH PIZZA

Chicago's deep-dish pizza is thick, like a pie, and baked in a skillet. It requires a fork and knife to eat because it's hard to pick up!

WILD ONIONS

Chicago takes its name from an Algonquin word meaning "smelly onion," a reference to the wild allium plants that once grew here.

BABY BACK RIBS

Many African-Americans migrated from the Mississippi Delta, and brought barbecue recipes and culture with them. Baby back pork ribs remain a local favorite.

SPRINGFIELD

★

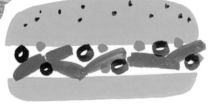

PIEROGIES

Illinois is home to nearly a million Polish-Americans. They make dumplings called pierogies—filled with potato, cheese, or cabbage.

HORSERADISH

Illinois is the horseradish capital of the world. The town of Collinsville celebrates its spicy crop by holding an annual contest to see who can throw a fresh horseradish root the farthest.

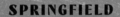

ITALIAN BEEF

Created near Chicago's famous stock yards, the Italian Beef is a messy, juicy roast beef sandwich.

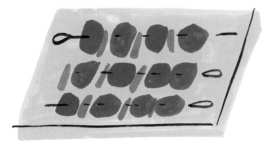

GREEK FOOD

Chicago is home to many residents of Greek ancestry. In the Greektown neighborhood, restaurants and diners serve gyro platters, lamb kabobs, spanakopita (spinach pie) and *saganaki* (flaming cheese).

69

Chicago-Style Hot Dogs

PREPARATION TIME	COOKING TIME	LEVEL OF DIFFICULTY	SERVES
5 minutes	10 minutes	● ○ ○	6

Across most of America, people top their hot dogs with ketchup and little else, but not in this state. The Chicago Dog is covered in so many veggies—chopped onions, sliced tomatoes, a crunchy dill pickle spear, plus a sprinkling of celery salt—that people lovingly say it's been "dragged through the garden." One thing you leave off a Chicago Dog? Ketchup!

INGREDIENTS
6 all-beef hot dogs
6 split hot dog rolls,
   preferably seeded
6 dill pickle spears
12 thin slices tomato
Yellow mustard
Sweet relish
1 small white onion, finely
   chopped
6 sport peppers or
   pepperoncini
Celery salt (optional)

1. Bring water to a boil in a medium saucepan, and then cook hot dogs in it until warmed through, 3–5 minutes.

2. Transfer the hot dogs to the rolls and place a pickle spear on one side of each hot dog and 2 tomato slices on the other side. Cover hot dogs with yellow mustard and relish. Sprinkle with chopped onion and top with a sport pepper. Sprinkle with celery salt, if desired, and serve.

Eating in INDIA

Indiana is home of the Indy 500 car race, but food here isn't fast or flashy. It's made by hand, cooked from the heart, and served with hometown pride.

Indiana is sandwiched between different regions. Maybe that's why Hoosiers (that's the nickname for Indiana residents) love sandwiches—Coney dogs, fried bologna, and even the fried brain sandwich, popular in the city of Evansville. The most beloved example is the Breaded Pork Tenderloin, or the BPT. A slice of tenderloin is pounded flat, coated in cornmeal, and fried until crisp and tender. It's served on bread with lettuce, tomato, mustard, and pickles. True Hoosiers order a root beer alongside.

Indiana dinners are unfussy and delicious. The state is landlocked, but its northwest corner borders Lake Michigan. Here, freshwater fish such as perch make a traditional Sunday supper. Down in Indianapolis, pan-fried chicken dinners are more common. Other state favorites include meat loaf with mashed potatoes, chicken with fresh egg noodles, roast beef with gravy, and smoked sausage with baked beans. They're served with piles of cheesy cauliflower, buttered corn, carrot-raisin slaw, creamy pea salad— and warm biscuits, too. For dessert, you'll find fruit cobbler, peppermint ice cream, or cream pie!

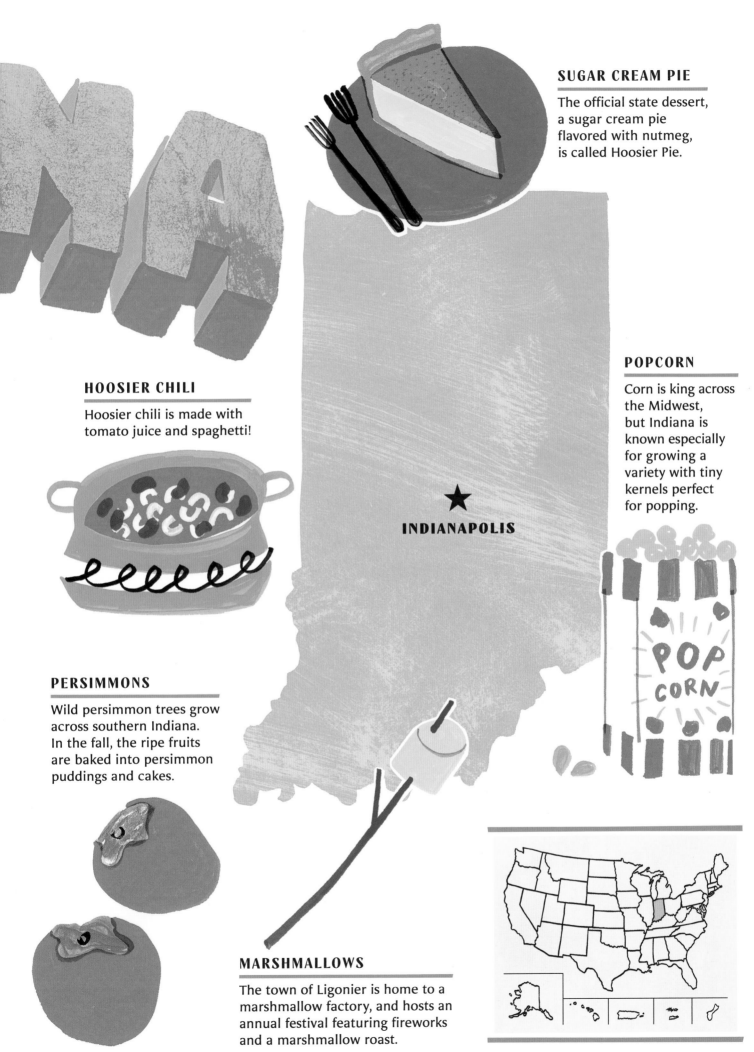

SUGAR CREAM PIE

The official state dessert, a sugar cream pie flavored with nutmeg, is called Hoosier Pie.

HOOSIER CHILI

Hoosier chili is made with tomato juice and spaghetti!

POPCORN

Corn is king across the Midwest, but Indiana is known especially for growing a variety with tiny kernels perfect for popping.

★

INDIANAPOLIS

PERSIMMONS

Wild persimmon trees grow across southern Indiana. In the fall, the ripe fruits are baked into persimmon puddings and cakes.

POP CORN

MARSHMALLOWS

The town of Ligonier is home to a marshmallow factory, and hosts an annual festival featuring fireworks and a marshmallow roast.

Fresh Egg Noodles

PREPARATION TIME	COOKING TIME	LEVEL OF DIFFICULTY	SERVES
45 minutes	10 minutes	●●○	6

Yes, you can go to the store and buy a package of dried egg noodles. But making them at home is a lot of fun—like working with Play-Doh. You just mix simple dough, roll it thin, slice it into thick strips, and boil it. Serve with some melted butter and chopped parsley, with roast chicken, or all on its own, and you may never go back to the package again! If you have a stand mixer, consider buying the pasta-rolling attachment. It makes rolling the dough as easy as boiling water!

INGREDIENTS

2 cups all-purpose flour, plus more for work surface
1 teaspoon salt
1 large egg
3 large egg yolks
Butter, for serving
Fresh flat-leaf parsley, chopped, for serving (optional)

1. In a medium bowl, whisk to combine the flour and salt. Make a well in the center and add the egg, egg yolks, and enough water to make the dough bendy and stretchy (about ¼ cup). Using a wooden spoon, mix thoroughly; if the dough feels dry, add a little more water.

2. Lightly flour a work surface, and turn out the dough onto it. Knead until smooth, adding flour as needed, about 2 minutes. Wrap with plastic and let rest at room temperature for 30 minutes.

3. With a rolling pin, roll the dough very thin on the lightly floured work surface. With a knife, cut into ½-inch wide strips and again into 6-inch lengths. Lightly sprinkle the noodles with flour to keep them from sticking together.

4. Bring a pot of water to a rapid boil. Stir in the noodles and boil until they rise to the top, about 3 minutes. Drain in a colander and transfer to a serving bowl. Toss with butter and chopped parsley, if using, and serve immediately.

Eating in IOWA

Nearly every acre of Iowa is farmland. That's thanks to the mile-thick glaciers that left behind some of the richest soil in the world. Today, corn and soybeans are the biggest crops, mostly grown to feed to livestock. In Iowa, pigs outnumber people seven to one! Iowans celebrate those pigs at the state fair each August in Des Moines, the capital. There you can listen to a hog-hollerin' contest (or join in—there's a youth category for ages 5 to 16), check out the big boar competition (past winners have weighed more than 1,300 pounds!), and enjoy a thick, juicy pork chop served on a stick.

Iowans also love to eat beef—especially in messy-but-delicious "loose meat" sandwiches called Maid-Rites, or in open-faced hot roast beef sandwiches topped with mashed potatoes and gravy. They also invented taco pizza, topped with refried beans, ground beef, cheese, lettuce, tomato, and crumbled tortilla chips. These only-in-Iowa favorites are sold at gas stations throughout the state, but those aren't the only roadside places Iowans buy dinner. Churches and 4-H Clubs set up stands selling sweet corn, popcorn, and pie. One popular pie filling is rhubarb, which looks like pink celery and is nicknamed "pie plant."

MAYTAG BLUE CHEESE

In 1941, Iowa State University microbiologists developed a new process for making cheese with blue swirls. Today, Maytag blue cheese is eaten in every state!

SAUERKRAUT

Several towns in Iowa celebrate sauerkraut days every summer, honoring the fermented cabbage.

DES MOINES

FISH AND RICE

Iowa is home to many Tai Dam immigrants from Southeast Asia. They introduced their delicious traditional dishes to the state, including fish and rice.

STATEWIDE BICYCLE RIDE

Every year, more than 10,000 people take part in the Great Bicycle Ride Across Iowa. They take breaks to eat pie, like sour cream raisin pie with meringue topping.

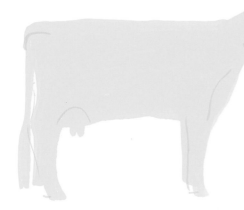

BUTTER COW

At the Iowa State Fair, visitors marvel at the Butter Cow, a life-sized cow sculpture made of 600 pounds of butter!

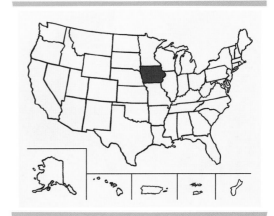

Creamed Corn

PREPARATION TIME	COOKING TIME	LEVEL OF DIFFICULTY	SERVES
10 minutes	20 minutes	● ○ ○	4

Iowa grows more corn than any other state, but more than 99 percent of it is something called field corn, to be turned into animal feed, ethanol, corn syrup, and more. (The stuff you love to eat on the cob is known as sweet corn.) Farmers say the plants should be "knee high by the Fourth of July," and the ears ripe for the picking in late summer, when the tassels turn dark brown. Sweet corn is pretty fantastic simply steamed and slathered with butter, but for a serious summer indulgence, simmer it with sugar, flour, butter, and cream.

INGREDIENTS
3 large ears of corn, husked
1 tablespoon sugar
1 tablespoon all-purpose
    flour
3 tablespoons unsalted
    butter, melted
1 cup heavy (whipping)
    cream
Salt and freshly ground
    black pepper

1. With a sharp knife, cut the kernels off the cobs and into a large bowl. (Work carefully, to prevent the cob from slipping. It can help to cut off the tip first, so it can sit flat while you hold the cob by the stem end.) Using the back of the knife blade, scrape the cobs to release all of the milk and any remaining bits of corn.

2. Toss the corn kernels with the sugar, flour, butter, and cream.

3. Transfer the corn mixture to a large skillet and cook over medium heat, stirring constantly, until very thick, about 20 minutes. Season to taste with salt and pepper. Serve hot.

Eating in KANS

Kansas's farmers grow so much wheat that the state is often called "America's Breadbasket." The wheat is milled into flour and shipped all over the country. All the wheat grown in Kansas each year could be used to bake 36 billion loaves of bread!

Summers here on the prairie are hot and dry, so farmers grow a variety known as winter wheat. It's planted in the fall and harvested in the spring or early summer. At busy harvest time, Kansan neighbors used to share the work by gathering to thresh the wheat, or separate the kernels of grain from the dry straw. Threshing dinners became important community gatherings, complete with roast beef, pies, and of course warm, home-baked bread.

Today, farms are bigger, and rather than thresh by hand, farmers rely on giant machines known as combine harvesters to gather the grain from the fields, often working late into the night. Because farms can cover miles and miles, families drive out to the fields and take turns driving the grain truck and sharing packed picnics. Meat loaf, Jell-O, and cinnamon rolls are all popular harvesttime foods. If all goes well, Kansans celebrate the end of the wheat harvest season on the Fourth of July, with big plates of barbecued beef followed by homemade ice cream.

CORN SOUP

The indigenous Kaw people prepared corn soup seasoned with bison meat and rock salt.

HOME ON THE RANGE

The state song, "Home on the Range," was written in a cabin near West Beaver Creek in 1872. People still sing it around campfires today, dreaming of a home "where the buffalo roam, and the deer and the antelope play."

★
TOPEKA

PANCAKES

Early settlers often cooked wheat flour into flapjacks as flat as the prairie. A major street in the city of Liberal is called Pancake Boulevard.

BARBECUE

For African-Americans leaving the South to pursue freedom after the Civil War, Kansas was the closest point in the North. They brought barbecue recipes along with their dreams of a new life.

SLIDERS

The itty-bitty snack-sized burgers called sliders were popularized in Wichita in the 1920s. Back then, five sliders cost just 25 cents!

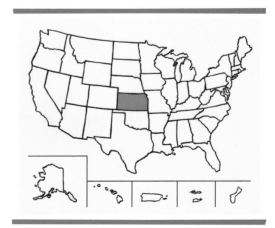

Classic American White Bread

PREPARATION TIME	COOKING TIME	LEVEL OF DIFFICULTY	MAKES
20 minutes, plus rising time	1 hour 10 minutes	● ● ○	2 loaves

Anyone can make a sandwich, but it feels pretty great to make the sandwich bread, too. As long as you follow the recipe, baking bread from scratch isn't complicated, and a fresh-from-the-oven loaf makes the whole house smell delicious.

INGREDIENTS
1½ cups milk
¼ cup sugar
6 tablespoons unsalted butter, plus more, softened, for bowl and loaf pans
1 (¼-ounce) packet active dry yeast (2¼ teaspoons)
2 large eggs
1 tablespoon salt
6–6½ cups all-purpose flour

SPECIAL EQUIPMENT
2 (9 x 5-inch) loaf pans

1. In a small saucepan, scald the milk over medium heat (bring it just to the point where it is *almost* at a boil). Remove from the heat and stir in the sugar and 3 tablespoons of the butter until the butter is melted and sugar is dissolved.

2. Pour into a large bowl and let cool to lukewarm (it should feel barely warm to the touch), and then stir in the yeast. Stir in the eggs. Add the salt and 4 cups of the flour. Beat with a wooden spoon until smooth, about 2 minutes. Add 2 more cups flour. The dough will become too stiff to stir, but work in as much flour as possible.

3. Flour a work surface, and turn the dough out onto it. Knead for 10 minutes, adding more flour if necessary, to make a smooth and elastic dough. Brush a large bowl with softened butter and place the dough in it, turning to coat it with butter. Cover with a damp kitchen towel and let the dough rise in a warm, draft-free area until doubled in volume, about 1½ hours.

4. Brush the loaf pans with softened butter. Punch down the dough. Divide it in half and form each half into a loaf shape; place each in a buttered pan. Cover with damp kitchen towels and let rise until dough is doubled in size, 45 minutes to 1 hour.

5. Position a rack in the middle of the oven and preheat to 350°F.

6. Bake until the bread is browned, 45 minutes to 1 hour. You can test if it's done baking by carefully removing a loaf from the pan and tapping it on the bottom; if it sounds hollow, it's done.

7. Remove the bread from the pans and place on a wire rack. Melt the remaining 3 tablespoons butter and brush over the tops of the warm bread, dividing evenly. Let bread cool completely before slicing.

Eating in KENTU

In Kentucky, it's all about the *B*'s: bluegrass, barbecue, and the famous whiskey known as bourbon. You have to be an adult to drink bourbon, but it's baked into lots of kid-friendly desserts, from cakes to pies. The Kentucky Derby, the horse race that's been drawing crowds to Louisville each spring since 1875, inspired a special chocolate pecan pie with a few drops of that famous bourbon.

People of all ages can sink their teeth into Kentucky barbecue. Choose pork, beef, chicken, or mutton (grown-up sheep). Baby back ribs are popular, served with bread, onion, and a pickle. It's best while listening to some bluegrass banjo!

The Bluegrass State (named for the native wild bluegrass that grows here, now also a name for its famous mountain music) has even more specialties that begin with *B*. There's the hunter's stew called burgoo. Benedictine sandwiches, made with a cucumber-and-cream cheese spread, are especially popular during horse race season. And the Hot Brown, an open-faced sandwich featuring turkey, bacon, and a creamy sauce, was first served as a late-night meal at The Brown Hotel in Louisville.

MUTTON

People across the South make barbecue with pork, chicken, or beef, but in Kentucky, they also barbecue sheep meat, known as mutton.

HAM BISCUIT

The annual ham festival in Trigg County includes the world's largest ham biscuit and the chance to kiss a pig!

★
FRANKFORT

THE ORIGINAL KFC

KFC (short for Kentucky Fried Chicken) started at a gas station in the city of Corbin and is now known around the world.

CHEESEBURGER

Some say that the first cheeseburger was served at Kaelin's Restaurant in Louisville in 1934.

BURGOO

Kentucky burgoo is a hunter's stew that can include any game meat hunters catch, such as venison, rabbit, quail, possum, or squirrel.

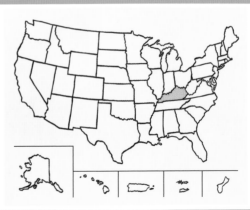

Oven-Fried Chicken

PREPARATION TIME	COOKING TIME	LEVEL OF DIFFICULTY	SERVES
15 minutes, plus 8 hours brining time	30 to 40 minutes	● ● ○	4

Deep-frying can be messy, but oven "frying" is much simpler and safer. This recipe makes use of an easy brine (or bath) to lock in the moisture, resulting in the most tender, flavorful chicken. It may seem like a long time to wait, but try it once and you'll see why it's worth it.

INGREDIENTS
Coarse salt
3 tablespoons sugar
4 chicken drumsticks
4 bone-in skin-on chicken thighs
1 cup all-purpose flour
½ cup cornmeal
1 teaspoon garlic powder
1 teaspoon paprika
1 cup buttermilk
Nonstick cooking spray or vegetable oil, for baking sheet

SPECIAL EQUIPMENT
an instant-read thermometer

1. To make the brine, combine 6 tablespoons salt, the sugar, and 4 cups cold water in a large bowl and stir until the sugar and salt dissolve in the water. Add another 4 cups cold water, and then add the chicken pieces. Cover and refrigerate, 8–12 hours. Then, remove the chicken from the brine, discard the brine, and pat the chicken pieces dry with paper towels.

2. Preheat the oven to 425°F. Line a large baking sheet with parchment paper and spray or brush lightly with oil.

3. In a shallow bowl, whisk to combine the flour, cornmeal, garlic powder, paprika, and ½ teaspoon salt. Pour the buttermilk into another shallow bowl.

4. Working in batches, dip the chicken in the buttermilk and then dip in the flour mixture, rolling it around until it's covered completely and shaking off the excess. Transfer the chicken pieces to the prepared baking sheet (skin side down for the thighs).

5. Roast the chicken, for 25 to 30 minutes, turning the pan around in the oven halfway through, until very brown on the bottom. Remove from oven. Working quickly, use tongs to flip the chicken pieces over. Return to oven and roast 5 to 10 minutes longer, until brown and an instant-read thermometer inserted into the thickest parts registers 165°F. Transfer chicken to a wire rack and let cool for at least 10 minutes. Serve hot or at room temperature. (Chicken can be covered and refrigerated for up to 2 days and served cold.)

Eating in LOUISIANA

This state's mix of cultures and people come together in one wonderful recipe: gumbo.

The name "gumbo" probably comes from a West African word meaning okra, the vegetable that makes the stew so nice and thick. Native Choctaw people contributed *file* powder, from ground sassafras leaves (the same plant that flavors root beer!). French settlers originally called Acadians, which came to be pronounced "Cajun," flavored gumbo with a butter-flour sauce cooked until it's deep red (it's called *roux,* from the French word for red). No wonder people call Louisiana a melting pot!

Louisiana is also called the Bayou State, for its brackish, boggy wetlands. These marshy bayous are home to crawfish, shrimp, frogs, turtles, and alligators, all of which Cajuns have cooked into pots of gumbo. Popular variations also include smoked chicken and a smoked sausage called andouille.

Gumbo is served over rice, which grows well along the wet banks of the mighty Mississippi River and across the Cajun prairies. Don't forget to season your bowl with a generous shake of hot sauce. Condiments made with vinegar and lots of hot peppers can be found on every table throughout the state!

HOT

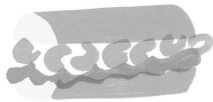

PO' BOY

The classic Louisiana sandwich most often features fried seafood (usually oysters or shrimp) tucked into French bread.

RED BEANS AND RICE

Many Creole cooks make red beans and rice for dinner every single Monday. The world-famous jazz musician Louis Armstrong, who grew up in Louisiana, used to sign his letters "Red beans and ricely yours," after his favorite dish.

CRAWFISH

Crawfish—also known as crayfish, crawdads, or mudbugs—look like tiny lobsters. Louisianans eat them boiled, broiled, or in a spicy Cajun stew called étouffée (pronounced AY-too-FAY).

GULF SHRIMP

Wild shrimp from the Gulf of Mexico are plump, tender, and sweet. Locals call them Louisiana gold, and include them in gumbo, jambalaya, and shrimp creole.

BANANAS FOSTER

Bananas Foster, invented at Brennan's Restaurant in New Orleans in the 1950s, is served in flames.

BATON ROUGE ★

MUFFULETTA

In 1906, a New Orleans grocer noticed Sicilian immigrants eating salami, provolone, olives, and bread for lunch. He combined them into the now-famous muffuletta sandwich.

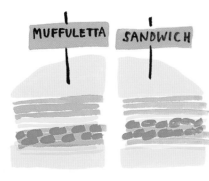

MUFFULETTA SANDWICH

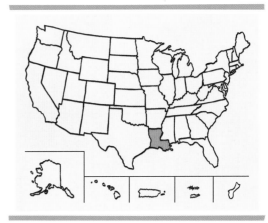

BEIGNETS

Beignets (pronounced bayn-YAY) are square dough fritters dusted with powdered sugar. Order them for breakfast (or dessert) at New Orleans's famous Café du Monde.

POWDERED SUGAR

Jambalaya

PREPARATION TIME	COOKING TIME	LEVEL OF DIFFICULTY	SERVES
20 minutes	55 minutes	● ● ●	8–10

Every spring, the city of New Orleans throws a wild party called Mardi Gras (that's French for "Fat Tuesday") when everyone eats this celebratory dish, but you can make it any day of the year. The name reflects its diverse influences and ingredients: French jambon (ham) and à la (meaning "with" or "on top of"), plus a West African word, ya, for rice. In Louisiana, you'll also find versions with chicken, shrimp, or spicy andouille sausage.

INGREDIENTS

3 tablespoons vegetable oil
¾ pound skinless, boneless chicken thighs
½ teaspoon salt
¼ teaspoon freshly ground black pepper
¾ pound smoked sausage, such as andouille, sliced
1 yellow onion, finely chopped
3 stalks celery, thinly sliced
1 large red bell pepper, finely chopped
4 cloves garlic, minced
1 bay leaf
1 tablespoon Creole seasoning
3 cups chopped tomatoes
3 cups chicken stock, preferably low-sodium
2 cups long-grain rice
1 pound medium shrimp, peeled and deveined
1 tablespoon fresh lemon juice
¼ cup chopped fresh flat-leaf parsley
¼ cup sliced scallions

1. Heat oil in a large Dutch oven over medium heat. Sprinkle salt and pepper on both sides of the chicken. Add chicken to the hot oil and cook, turning over occasionally, until cooked through, about 10 minutes. Remove the chicken and set pan aside. Once the chicken is cool enough to handle, shred into 1-inch pieces.

2. Return the pan to medium heat, add the sausage, and cook for 5 minutes, turning once. Transfer the sausage to a plate and leave the fat in the pan. Add the onion, celery, bell pepper, garlic, bay leaf, and Creole seasoning, and cook until the vegetables are softened and the onion is translucent, 5–7 minutes. Stir in the tomatoes, stock, and rice and return the chicken and sausage to the pan. Bring to a boil over medium-high heat. Cover the pan; reduce the heat to medium-low, and simmer, stirring occasionally, until the rice is tender, about 20 minutes.

3. Top rice mixture with the shrimp, cover, and cook just until the shrimp turn pink, about 5 minutes. Stir in the lemon juice, parsley, and scallions. Serve immediately.

Eating in MAINE

Maine has one of the smallest populations of any state, perhaps because few people can brave its long, bitterly cold winters. But in summer, Maine is such a popular place to visit that it's nicknamed "Vacationland." When school lets out, families from all over come to enjoy the Atlantic coastline, known for its charming towns, lighthouses, whale watching, and of course, its food!

Maine's northern climate is too cold for year-round farming, but wild blueberries grow very happily—more here than in any other state. Summer visitors eat them in muffins or pie, or right off the bushes on forest hikes. But if there's one food for which Maine is best known, it's lobster.

Maine's "lobstahmen" trap the giant shellfish in the cold Atlantic waters and ship them all over the world. In Maine, people eat lobster on hot dog buns with mayonnaise, in bowls of chowder, baked into macaroni and cheese, or just cracked open and dipped in melted butter. This can be so messy that even grown-ups wear special lobster bibs!

POUTINE

Up near the Canadian border, some Maine families cook French-Canadian recipes like poutine—French fries topped with cheese and gravy.

POTATO DONUTS

Potatoes have been Maine's biggest crop for two hundred years. Mainers put them in everything—even donuts!

MOOSE

Mainers cook moose chili, roast moose, and moose meatballs from the wild moose that they hunt in local forests.

AUGUSTA

CLAMS AND LOBSTER

Maine is famous for lobster, but clams aren't far behind. Mainers enjoy fried clams, clam chowder, clam rolls, and even clam burgers.

Whoopie Pies

WHOOPIE PIES

Mainers enjoy unique desserts called whoopie pies, which are not pies at all but soft cookie-and-frosting sandwiches. (People in Pennsylvania also claim to have invented whoopie pies, but Mainers say that's baloney!)

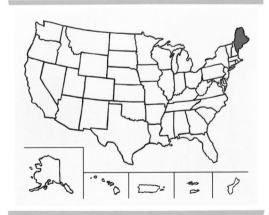

Blueberry Muffins

PREPARATION TIME	**COOKING TIME**	**LEVEL OF DIFFICULTY**	**MAKES**
15 minutes	25 minutes	● ○ ○	12 muffins

Summer mornings in Maine mean muffins filled with fresh blueberries picked the day before. You can use frozen wild berries to enjoy a taste of Vacationland all year round. Whichever berries you use, toss them with a tablespoon of the flour before folding into the batter, to keep them from sinking to the bottom as the muffins bake.

INGREDIENTS

2 cups all-purpose flour
1 teaspoon baking powder
½ teaspoon baking soda
¼ teaspoon freshly grated nutmeg
½ teaspoon salt
1 stick unsalted butter, melted
¾ cup granulated sugar
2 large eggs
1 teaspoon pure vanilla extract
½ cup buttermilk
2¼ cups blueberries
1-2 tablespoons turbinado sugar, for topping (optional)

1. Position a rack in the middle of the oven and preheat to 375°F. Grease 12 cups of a muffin tin or line with cupcake papers.

2. In a large bowl, whisk together the flour, baking powder, baking soda, nutmeg, and salt.

3. In another bowl, whisk the melted butter with the sugar. Whisk in the eggs, one at a time, and combine well. Stir in the vanilla and buttermilk. Pour the wet ingredients into the flour mixture and stir well to combine. Fold in the blueberries.

4. Scoop the batter into the muffin cups. Sprinkle evenly with turbinado sugar, if desired. Bake until the muffin tops are golden brown and a skewer inserted into the center comes out clean, 20–25 minutes. Let the muffins cool slightly in the pan, until they are cool enough to handle, and then transfer to a wire rack. Serve warm or at room temperature.

Eating in MARYLAND

Maryland was named for Henrietta Maria, a queen consort to King Charles I. These days, it's better known as the state where *crab* is king.

Maryland's miles of coastline and vast Chesapeake Bay are the perfect habitat for this crustacean. Blue crabs are so plentiful that many people make their living as crabbers. Some crabbers catch them using a chicken bone tied to a rope. Pretty much anywhere you go out to eat in Maryland, crab is on the menu. Simple crab shacks and fancy restaurants alike serve freshly caught blue crab, boiled or steamed, with melted butter for dipping. It's messy work to crack the shell and carefully pick out the insides, but the reward is a plate piled high with sweet, briny crabmeat. Families often sit around "cracking crab" on a picnic table near the beach, eating and talking for hours.

In the summer months, you can eat crab whole—shell and all! Some locals keep their catch in tanks to watch and wait for just this softshell moment, before the new shell hardens. The "softies" are battered and pan-fried, or stuffed into sandwiches, with lettuce, tomato, and mayo. Without them, Marylanders can get very crabby!

AND

LAKE TROUT SANDWICH

The lake trout sandwich (actually made with ocean-caught whiting!) is a popular take-out meal in Baltimore.

FRIED CHICKEN WITH GRAVY

Maryland fried chicken has a crisp, thin crust. Locals drizzle it with peppery cream gravy.

LEXINGTON PUBLIC MARKET

Baltimore's Lexington Public Market is the longest-running public market in the country, established way back in 1782.

★ ★ ★ WORLD FAMOUS ★ ★ ★ LEXINGTON MARKET SINCE 1782

SMITH ISLAND CAKE

This cake, named for Maryland's Smith Island, is the state's official dessert. It features up to 15 super-thin layers, each separated by fudge frosting.

ANNAPOLIS

BLUE CRAB

Maryland's most famous food is the blue crab from the Chesapeake Bay.

Smith Island Cake

OLD BAY

This seasoning is a blend of celery salt, pepper, and paprika. People in Maryland shake it onto fries, eggs, corn on the cob, and of course, crab.

OLD BAY SEASONING
For Seafood Poultry, Salads, Meats
Same great taste for over 75 years
NET WT 6 OZ   170 g

PIT BEEF

Try a hometown favorite while you watch a Baltimore Orioles game—a sandwich piled high with finely shaved, fire-roasted pit beef and topped with horseradish and raw onions.

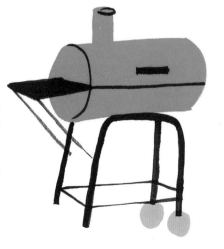

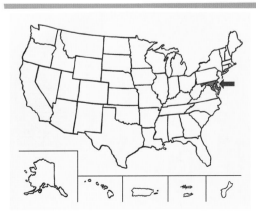

Crab Cakes

PREPARATION TIME	COOKING TIME	LEVEL OF DIFFICULTY	SERVES
10 minutes, plus 1 hour chilling time	15 minutes	● ● ○	4

If you've only tasted crab cakes that came from a landlocked freezer, you haven't really tasted crab cakes! The real thing uses lots of fresh, succulent crab with a tender texture and unbeatable taste. Enjoy them with tangy tartar sauce on the side, or make it a meal on a toasted bun.

INGREDIENTS
1 pound lump crabmeat, picked over, any bits of shells and cartilage discarded
2 slices white sandwich bread, crusts removed
1 large egg, lightly beaten
2 tablespoons minced white onion
2 teaspoons Dijon mustard
1 teaspoon Worcestershire sauce
2 teaspoons Old Bay seasoning
4 tablespoons butter
1 lemon, cut into wedges, for serving

SPECIAL EQUIPMENT
a food processor

1. Using a fork or your fingers, break the crabmeat into smaller pieces and place in a large bowl. Tear the bread into pieces and pulse in a food processor just until coarse (not fine) crumbs are formed; add to the crab. Stir in the beaten egg, then the onion, mustard, Worcestershire sauce, and Old Bay. Cover and refrigerate for at least 1 hour to chill.

2. Dividing evenly, form the mixture into 8 small patties. Heat a large skillet over medium-high heat. Add the butter and let melt, then add the crab cakes and cook until light golden brown on the bottom, about 5 minutes. Flip gently and cook until the other side is light golden brown, about 5 minutes. Serve with lemon wedges.

Eating in MASSACHU...

Massachusetts has almost 200 miles of coastline, so locals have always feasted on seafood—especially clams. In fact, Native people have eaten this mollusk for more than 2,000 years! Bay Staters love baked clams, stuffed clams, clam cakes, fried clam bellies and strips, creamy clam chowder served with oyster crackers, and pasta with clams and garlic.

Eating clams is even more fun when you dig for them yourself! For generations, professional and amateur clam diggers have waded out into the shallow coastal waters to harvest different kinds of clams from the sandy muck: quahogs (for chowder and stuffed clams), steamers (to steam and then dip into bowls of melted butter), cherrystones (for grilling), and littlenecks (to shuck and slurp raw).

With wire baskets overflowing with clams, friends gather for traditional clambakes right on the beach, cooking the clams in a pit layered with sand, seaweed, and fire-warmed stones, alongside lobsters, potatoes, and corn on the cob. If you get a chance to join this kind of beachside feast, you may just find yourself as happy as a clam.

CODFISH

New Englanders have been catching cod for more than 400 years. They cook the mild, sweet fish into codfish cakes, chowders, and sandwiches.

CRANBERRIES

Cranberries, the state fruit of Massachusetts, grow on low-lying vines in wetlands called bogs. At harvest time, farmers flood the bogs, so they can easily skim the ripe berries from the surface.

BOSTON CREAM PIE

Despite its name, Boston cream pie is a *cake*, first made at the city's Parker House Hotel in 1856.

Boston Cream Pie

★
BOSTON

PANCAKES

The world's largest pancake breakfast is held every year in the city of Springfield. They use more than 500 gallons of batter to make the pancakes, which get topped with 4,700 pounds of butter and 450 gallons of maple syrup!

BOSTON BAKED BEANS

Boston is called Beantown for its famous baked beans, served alongside round brown bread that is steamed in a coffee can.

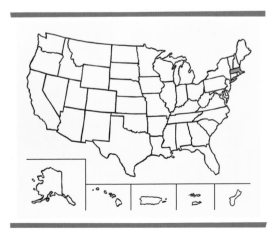

MA

Chocolate Chip Cookies

PREPARATION TIME	COOKING TIME	LEVEL OF DIFFICULTY	MAKES
15 minutes	30 minutes	● ○ ○	30 cookies

Chocolate chip cookies were invented by accident in the 1930s, when Ruth Wakefield, the cook at the Toll House Inn in the town of Whitman, tried to make chocolate cookies by adding chopped chocolate chunks to her dough. Instead of melting, the chips kept their shape, and America's favorite cookie was born! This recipe is a variation on the classic.

INGREDIENTS
2¼ cups all-purpose flour
1 teaspoon baking soda
½ teaspoon baking powder
1 teaspoon coarse salt
2 sticks unsalted butter, room temperature
½ cup granulated sugar
¾ cup packed light brown sugar
1 teaspoon pure vanilla extract
2 large eggs
1 (12-ounce) bag semisweet chocolate chips (2 cups)
1 cup chopped walnuts or pecans (optional)

1. Preheat the oven to 375°F.

2. In a bowl, whisk together the flour, baking soda, baking powder, and salt.

3. With an electric mixer, beat the butter and both sugars together until light and fluffy, 3-5 minutes. Beat in the vanilla. Beat in the eggs, 1 at a time. On low speed, beat in the flour mixture just until combined. Fold in the chocolate chips and nuts (if using).

4. Line 2 large baking sheets with parchment paper. Drop the dough by rounded tablespoons onto the lined sheets, spacing 2 inches apart (they will spread while baking). Bake until golden brown, about 14 minutes, rotating sheets and switching racks halfway though. Let the cookies cool on the baking sheet for 2 minutes, then transfer to a wire rack to cool completely. Cookies can be stored in an airtight container at room temperature up to 5 days.

Eating in MICHIG[AN]

Detroit is nicknamed Motown. That's short for "motor town," because for more than a hundred years, the city has been home to America's biggest automakers. Their factories needed thousands of workers to make all those cars, so people came from around the world. And *that* made Michigan a delicious place to eat!

The Great Migration of African-Americans from the South and toward good factory jobs meant that Motor City was powered by soul food. Southern barbecue, collard greens, mac and cheese, and cornbread also powered the *music* of Motown. Some of the best soul food in America is still served in African-American churches or by backyard grill masters in Detroit.

Later, immigrants came from Lebanon, Syria, Yemen, and other parts of the Arab-speaking world to work at the factories. They brought foods such as shawarma, gyros, and baklava. Today, the largest Arab-American population in the US is in Michigan, so swing by a local deli for hummus, olives, and falafel!

Like a car assembled in the USA with parts from around the world, Detroit is flavored with *paczki* jelly donuts from Poland, rye bread from Jewish delis, *pupusas* from El Salvador, curry from India, and rich, flaky spanakopita from Greece.

CHERRIES

Cherries are big business in Michigan, home to more than four million cherry trees. Local orchards are especially famous for so-called sour cherries, the type baked into pies.

CORNISH PASTY

When miners arrived in Michigan from Cornwall, England, in the 1800s, they packed a traditional lunch that's still enjoyed today: the Cornish pasty, a handheld meat pie.

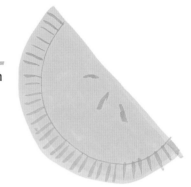

CONEY DOG

Although Coney Island is in New York, Michigan's famous Coney dogs (introduced by New Yorkers who moved here) are topped with chili, ground beef, and onions.

WHITEFISH

Locals enjoy fresh fish from the Great Lakes. Whitefish, named for its tender, mild meat, is popular in fried fish-and-chips, or smoked and mixed with mayonnaise to "schmear" on bagels.

THE REUBEN

Zingerman's Deli in Ann Arbor is the pride of the Midwest. Lines for sandwiches (the Reuben, featuring hot corned beef, sauerkraut, and Swiss cheese, is most popular) can stretch an hour or more.

LANSING ★

DETROIT-STYLE PIZZA

Detroit-style pizza has a thick, spongy crust and is served in square slices.

RYE BREAD

Michiganders love double-baked rye bread, especially when piled with slices of corned beef. The second baking brings an extra crunchy crust to each loaf.

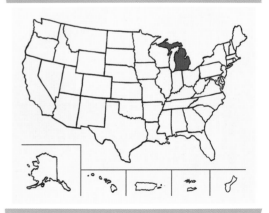

Tabbouleh

PREPARATION TIME	LEVEL OF DIFFICULTY	SERVES
35 minutes	● ○ ○	4–6

This summery salad is super refreshing, thanks to lots of parsley, mint, and lemon juice. Serve it with hummus, pita bread, and lamb burgers for a Middle Eastern feast, or alongside grilled chicken or fish.

INGREDIENTS

1½ cups finely chopped tomatoes (from about 2 medium)

¼ cup fine bulgur wheat

4 bunches fresh flat-leaf parsley

1 bunch fresh mint

4 scallions, trimmed and finely chopped

1 teaspoon coarse salt

¼ teaspoon freshly ground black pepper

⅓ cup extra-virgin olive oil

¼ cup fresh lemon juice

Romaine lettuce or green cabbage leaves (optional), for serving

1. In a large bowl, stir together the tomatoes (and all of their juices) and the bulgur wheat. Let rest for 20 minutes.

2. Meanwhile, remove the larger stems from the parsley and mint (small to medium stems are okay). Finely chop the parsley and place in a medium bowl. Finely chop the mint and add to the parsley along with the scallions.

3. Just before serving, combine the herb mixture with the tomato mixture. Season with the salt and pepper and stir in the olive oil and lemon juice. Serve with lettuce or cabbage leaves, if desired.

Eating in MINNE...

Minnesota is landlocked, but you could say it's got plenty of shoreline. That's because when the glaciers receded ten thousand years ago, they carved out the Great Lakes, including Lake Superior, the largest freshwater lake in the world. No wonder the Dakota Sioux named this land Minnesota, which means "clear blue waters." Today, the state is nicknamed the "Land of Ten Thousand Lakes."

People in Minnesota love to go fishing for walleye, the state fish, as well as muskies, crappies, and pike. They serve these fish fried, with a side of coleslaw and boiled red potatoes. In winter, locals don't let the cold stop them. Once the ice is thick enough, pickup trucks drive icehouses onto frozen lakes. Then, they hack holes through the deep ice, lower hooks into the water, and wait for the fish to bite. Some icehouses have heaters, beds, and TVs; on a Sunday, a whole village of icehouses might tune in to watch the Vikings play football!

Minnesota also has 70,000 miles of rivers (that's almost long enough to go around the earth three times!), including the headwaters of the mighty Mississippi. These rivers are home to trout and often bordered by bushes of gooseberries, a favorite in summertime pies.

...SOTA

SAMBUSAS

The Twin Cities are home to North America's largest community of people from Somalia, in East Africa. They make triangular meat-filled pastries called *sambusas*.

BUNDT CAKE

In 1950, a Minnesota metal expert made a specially shaped pan like one Jewish immigrants used to bake *kugelhopf* (a traditional German cake). The Bundt pan was born!

WILD RICE

Native Americans, including the Ojibwa, harvested wild rice by hand from canoes on the northern lakes. Today, you can still enjoy this wild food, which is actually a grass related to rice.

ST. PAUL ★

PORKETTA SANDWICH

Minnesota's special sandwiches include the porketta (made of shredded pork) and the Juicy Lucy (a burger with cheese *inside* the patty).

NORWEGIAN TREATS

Many Norwegian and Swedish immigrants came to Minnesota in the 1800s. Their descendants still serve lutefisk (made from dried cod), lefse (a gigantic flatbread), meatballs with lingonberry jam, St. Lucia Buns, and Norwegian wedding cakes (*Kransekake*), made of tasty almond-flavored rings.

Wild Rice Hotdish

PREPARATION TIME	COOKING TIME	LEVEL OF DIFFICULTY	SERVES
10 minutes	1 hour	● ● ○	4

In the Midwest, and especially in Minnesota, "hotdish" is the name for all kinds of baked casseroles that are popular at church suppers, potlucks, and family reunions, served straight from the baking dish. This version includes the state's special wild rice.

INGREDIENTS

1 package (6 ounces) long-grain white and wild rice mix, unseasoned
2 tablespoons butter
½ cup finely chopped onion
½ cup finely chopped celery
2 tablespoons all-purpose flour
2½ cups chicken stock, preferably low sodium
1 teaspoon chopped fresh thyme leaves or ½ teaspoon dried
½ cup sour cream
2 cups diced cooked chicken or turkey
Salt and freshly ground black pepper
¼ cup finely grated Parmesan cheese

SPECIAL EQUIPMENT

a fine-mesh sieve

1. Preheat the oven to 350°F. Butter a 4-quart deep baking dish.

2. Rinse the rice mix in a fine-mesh sieve.

3. In a large pot, melt the butter over medium heat. Add the onion and celery and cook, stirring, just until the onions are translucent, about 4 minutes. Stir in the flour. Add the chicken stock and bring to a simmer. Remove from the heat and stir in the rice mix, thyme, and sour cream until combined. Stir in the chicken or turkey and season to taste with salt and pepper.

4. Pour the mixture into the buttered baking dish. Cover tightly and bake for 35 minutes. Uncover, sprinkle with the Parmesan cheese, and bake, uncovered, until the top is golden brown, about 15 minutes. Serve immediately.

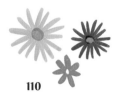

Eating in MISSISS...

Here's a riddle every kid in Mississippi can answer: *What kind of fish catches a mouse?*

If you answered *catfish,* bingo! Catfish (which don't really catch mice) are named for the whiskery-looking barbels on their noses. They have many nicknames, like chuckleheads, pollywogs, and mudcats. But no matter what people call them, nearly everyone loves to eat them.

Wild catfish thrive in the dark bottoms of Mississippi lakes, rivers, and streams. In the 1960s, Mississippians started raising the fish in ponds. Today, if you order catfish anywhere in America, it likely grew up in this state. Or you can come try to catch a wild one yourself the old-fashioned way—catfish are said to take almost any bait, including bubble gum, SPAM, and even soap!

In Mississippi, catfish is served baked, sautéed, fried, stewed, smoked, stuffed, and barbecued. Some fillets are dipped in spiced cornmeal, then fried and sandwiched on a baguette with lettuce and tomato to make po' boys, the unofficial sandwich of the Magnolia State. They're served all day at the World Catfish Festival, held each spring in the town of Belzoni, where you can watch a catfish-eating contest and the crowning of Miss Catfish.

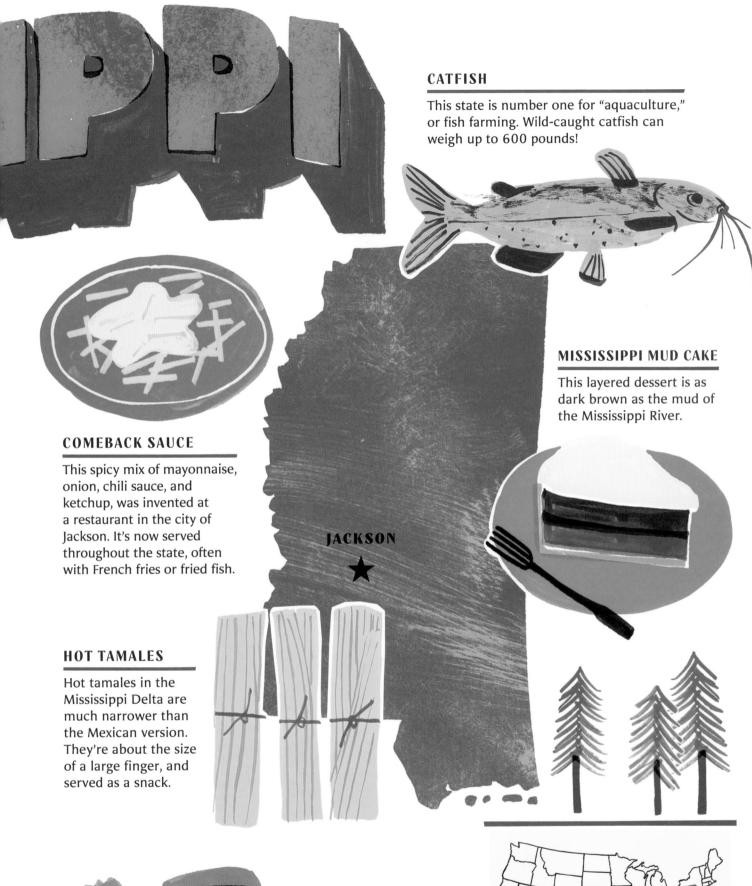

...IPPI

CATFISH

This state is number one for "aquaculture," or fish farming. Wild-caught catfish can weigh up to 600 pounds!

COMEBACK SAUCE

This spicy mix of mayonnaise, onion, chili sauce, and ketchup, was invented at a restaurant in the city of Jackson. It's now served throughout the state, often with French fries or fried fish.

MISSISSIPPI MUD CAKE

This layered dessert is as dark brown as the mud of the Mississippi River.

HOT TAMALES

Hot tamales in the Mississippi Delta are much narrower than the Mexican version. They're about the size of a large finger, and served as a snack.

JACKSON ★

PECANS

Mississippi grows towering pecan trees. People argue over to how to pronounce the nut's name, but everyone agrees they're delicious.

Oven-Fried Catfish

PREPARATION TIME	**COOKING TIME**	**LEVEL OF DIFFICULTY**	**SERVES**
5 minutes, plus 30 minutes soaking time	15 minutes	● ● ○	2

Many Mississippians like their catfish deep-fried, but a quick bake in the oven is much easier at home, and the cornmeal means you'll still get a nice crisp coating. Serve the fish straight from the oven, or pop in into a sandwich slathered with Mississippi's favorite condiment: comeback sauce.

INGREDIENTS

1 pound catfish fillets
1 cup milk
1 cup cornmeal
¼ cup all-purpose flour
1 teaspoon coarse salt
Freshly ground black pepper (optional)
Nonstick cooking spray or vegetable oil
Lemon wedges and tartar sauce, for serving

1. Preheat the oven to 425°F.

2. Cut catfish fillets into 3- or 4-inch pieces. Place in a medium bowl, add the milk, and let soak in the refrigerator for 30 minutes.

3. In another bowl, whisk together the cornmeal, flour, and salt. Season with black pepper, if desired. Line a large baking sheet with parchment paper and spray or brush lightly with oil.

4. Drain the fillet pieces and dip into the cornmeal, rolling them around until they're covered completely, then shaking off the excess. Transfer to the prepared baking sheet. Spray or very lightly brush the fillet pieces with more oil. Bake for about 7 minutes, until the undersides start to turn golden brown, then flip the fillet pieces and bake until cooked through, about 7 minutes longer.

5. Serve with lemon wedges and tartar sauce.

Eating in MISSO

A girl from the middle of the Midwest grew up to write the most famous cookbook in America. Irma Rombauer was born in St. Louis in 1877 and soaked up Midwest flavors: a crossroads of immigrants, African-Americans, and pioneer spirit. She loved baking, especially cakes with flowery frosting. She didn't love recipes that took all day—she liked to enjoy the party, too!

Irma decided to write a cookbook, and in 1931 she published 3,000 copies of *The Joy of Cooking*. Little did she know the book would end up in kitchens from coast to coast.

Irma's book showed American food in a time of change. It included recipes for farm foods, like pickles, pie, and even possum! But *The Joy of Cooking* also included recipes for canned ingredients, which many people saw as the foods of the future. Readers loved that Irma told jokes and stories like a good friend in the kitchen. She explained kitchen science, too.

Today, *The Joy of Cooking* has sold nearly 20 million copies! It became one of the most influential books of the 20th century, and millions of dishes, from meat loaf to mashed potatoes to chocolate cake, have been served thanks to our Missourian friend in the kitchen.

HOT SALAMI SANDWICH

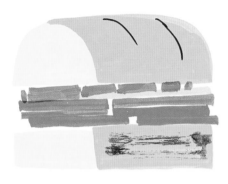

The hot salami sandwich from Gioia's Deli has been a St. Louis favorite for a century. Enjoy it with mustard.

BLACK WALNUTS

Each fall, people in Missouri gather black walnuts that fall from trees in the Ozark Mountains. Though tough to crack, they reward you with amazing flavor.

JEFFERSON CITY

STEAK

Cowboys used to bring cattle from the southwest to the Kansas City rail yards. Ever since, Kansas City (the one in Missouri) has been known for beef, including steak, barbecued brisket, and a local favorite called the "burnt ends."

TOASTED RAVIOLI

In St. Louis, Italian immigrants created toasted ravioli, which is fried instead of boiled.

PARTRIDGE

When writer Mark Twain, raised in the city of Hannibal, visited Europe in the late 1800s, he wrote a list of the American foods he missed, including broiled Missouri partridge, possum, and raccoon.

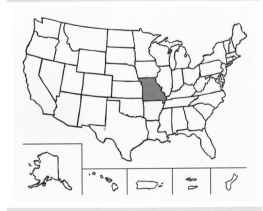

St. Louis Gooey Butter Cake

PREPARATION TIME	COOKING TIME	LEVEL OF DIFFICULTY	SERVES
10 minutes	30 minutes	● ○ ○	8–10

The measurements in this cake are all wrong if you're trying to bake a regular cake, but right on if you're trying to make a creamy-on-the-inside and crisp-on-the-sugary-top treat. This recipe came about by accident, when a new employee at a German bakery mixed up the measurements for a coffee cake. The finished cake was almost thrown out, but one taste changed everyone's minds. People in St. Louis have been baking it this way—on purpose—ever since!

INGREDIENTS

For the crust:
1 cup all-purpose flour
¼ cup granulated sugar
½ teaspoon salt
1 stick cold unsalted butter
1 large egg

For the filling:
1½ sticks unsalted butter, room temperature
1 cup granulated sugar
1 large egg
1 cup all-purpose flour
⅔ cup evaporated milk
¼ cup light corn syrup
1½ teaspoons pure vanilla extract
Powdered sugar, for dusting

1. Position a rack in the middle of the oven and preheat to 350°F. Butter an 8-inch square baking pan.

2. Make the crust: In a large bowl, whisk to combine the flour, granulated sugar, and salt. Using a pastry blender or two butter knives, quickly work the cubes of butter into the flour mixture until small crumbs form. Using a fork, stir in the egg. Press dough evenly into the bottom of the buttered pan.

3. Make the filling: In a medium bowl, beat the butter and granulated sugar with an electric mixer until light and fluffy. Add the egg and blend thoroughly. Alternately add the flour and evaporated milk. Beat in the corn syrup and vanilla until smooth.

4. Pour the batter over the crust. Bake until just set, 25–30 minutes. Transfer to a wire rack. Let the cake cool in the pan and dust with powdered sugar before slicing into squares and serving.

Eating in MONT

If you're lucky enough to visit Montana, you are probably headed to one of the state's magnificent national parks. Whether you're visiting Bighorn Canyon, Yellowstone, or Glacier National Park, the best way to experience them is with all five senses—including taste!

The state was named for the Spanish word for mountains (*montañas*). Now it's known as Big Sky Country, home to millions of acres of public land where people enjoy some of the best hunting and fishing in the world. You can track elk, deer, antelope, pheasant, geese, and turkey, the wild game that explorers Lewis and Clark ate here two hundred years ago. Early settlers in Montana were careful to use everything they could from each animal. A cookbook published in the city of Butte in 1900 featured "Calf's Head Soup!" Today, at some parks and historic sites, like Fort Union Trading Post, you can learn the frontier-cooking techniques fur trappers used, and get a true taste of the past.

CINNAMON ROLL

Cinnamon rolls are big in Montana—literally. Locals bake them bigger than burgers, using the hard, red wheat that grows well in the state's dry climate.

CHINESE FOOD

Chinese immigrants came to Montana mining towns in the late 18th century. They opened businesses in frontier towns, including many noodle shops.

HELENA

NOODLE SHOP

HUCKLEBERRIES

Summer is huckleberry season in Montana. They're cooked into pies and folded into ice cream. If you're picking them by the bucketful, you'll probably eat a lot right off the bush.

TROUT

People travel from all over the world to go fly-fishing for trout in Montana's beautiful freshwater rivers and streams. After a successful day of fishing, they eat pan-fried trout for dinner!

PULSES

Montana grows more pulses (dried seeds of legume plants, including lentils) than any other state.

BUFFALO

Many Native Americans in Montana relied on buffalo herds for food until their near-extinction in the late 19th century.

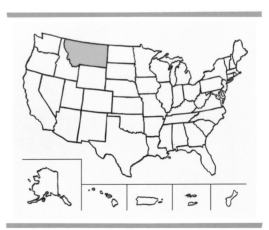

Blackberry Buckle

PREPARATION TIME	COOKING TIME	LEVEL OF DIFFICULTY	SERVES
15 minutes	45 minutes	● ○ ○	8–10

A buckle is a homey, old-fashioned fruit dessert, similar to a cobbler, crisp, or crumble. The fruit is folded into a buttery cake batter, which gets topped with cinnamon-and-sugar streusel before it's baked. You can use any fruit you like in a buckle, but blackberries are a popular choice in the Northern Rockies.

INGREDIENTS

For the batter:

1 stick unsalted butter, softened, plus more for pan
2 cups all-purpose flour, plus more for pan
1 teaspoon baking powder
½ teaspoon baking soda
½ teaspoon salt
¼ teaspoon freshly grated nutmeg
¾ cup sugar
1 large egg
½ cup buttermilk
2 cups blackberries

For the topping:

½ cup sugar
½ cup all-purpose flour
½ teaspoon ground cinnamon
¼ teaspoon salt
4 tablespoons unsalted butter, melted

1. Position a rack in the middle of the oven and preheat to 350°F. Brush a 9-inch cake pan with softened butter and dust with flour, shaking out excess.

2. Make the batter: In a medium bowl, whisk to combine the flour, baking powder, baking soda, salt, and nutmeg. In a large bowl, beat the butter and sugar with an electric mixer until light and fluffy, 3–5 minutes. Add the egg and mix well. Add the flour mixture in three additions, alternating with the buttermilk in two additions, beginning and ending with the flour. (In other words, add in a third of the flour, half the buttermilk, another third of the flour, the other half of the buttermilk, then the last third of the flour.) Stir well to combine.

3. With a flexible spatula, gently fold in the blackberries. Transfer the batter into the cake pan, and smooth the top with the spatula.

4. Make the topping: In a small bowl, whisk together the sugar, flour, cinnamon, and salt. With a fork, stir in the melted butter to form small clumps.

5. Sprinkle the topping evenly over the batter. Bake until a skewer inserted in the center comes out clean, about 45 minutes. Transfer to a wire rack to cool. Serve buckle warm.

Eating in NEBRA...

Nebraska grows a *lot* of corn, so the annual fall harvest is the busiest time of year. That's when the crop has to be husked and shucked from the cobs. Today, machines do this work, but for generations, Nebraska farmers hired extra help—called "cornhuskers"—for the harvest. Cornhusking meet-ups were part competition and part celebration. Champion huskers could shuck thousands of pounds of corn a day! That's how Nebraska got its nickname: the Cornhusker State.

Today, Nebraska harvests as much as a billion bushels of corn each year! And University of Nebraska fans know that harvesttime is also football season. The team is called the Cornhuskers, too! When you go to a game, hot dogs are shot out of a cannon into the crowd, but you'll probably want to buy them from the concession stand . . . the ones from the cannon explode on impact! At the century-old University of Nebraska Dairy Store, young food scientists make and sell cheese, ice cream, and other treats, all from corn-fed dairy cows.

From July through September, roadside stands sell bushels of the freshest corn around. The Omaha farmers' market grills Mexican-style corn on the cob. And inspired chefs make corn fritters, corn soup, and for dessert, sweet corn pudding.

SKA

RUNZA

The *runza*, a handheld pie of meat and vegetables baked in bread dough, was a common lunch a century ago. Today, it's a popular type of fast food at drive-through restaurants.

KOLACHE PASTRIES

Czech immigrants brought fruit-filled sweet pastries called *kolaches* to Nebraska. These days, annual festivals celebrate Czech foods in the cities of Verdigre and Wilber.

WILD PLUMS

Native Americans of the Great Plains, such as the Omaha and Kiowa, enjoyed wild plums. Today, Nebraskans still cook them into sweet jams and baked goods.

LINCOLN ★

CHEESE FRENCHEE

This grilled cheese sandwich is breaded in cornflakes and deep-fried.

STUFFED GRAPE LEAVES

Iraqi refugees introduced their new Nebraska neighbors to foods that included biryani (a mixed rice dish), stuffed grape leaves, and baklava.

SUDANESE FOOD

Omaha is home to America's largest group of people from the South Sudan in Africa. Their cuisine includes delicious meat stews, a thick savory porridge called *asida*, and creamy peanut sauces.

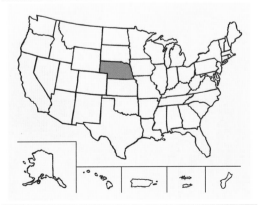

Popcorn Balls

PREPARATION TIME	COOKING TIME	LEVEL OF DIFFICULTY	MAKES
15 minutes	5 minutes	● ● ○	twelve 3-inch balls

An old legend says that Nebraska's intense sun and rain caused the first popcorn balls to form right in the field. While this tall tale can't be true, it is a fact that Nebraska grows excellent popping corn, and that people have been coating the popped kernels with sweet syrup for over a century. Be careful working with the syrup, which gets very hot. You'll be rewarded with a sweet-salty snack of candied corn balls that will be gone faster than you can say "Nebraska!"

INGREDIENTS
4 tablespoons butter, softened, plus more for the pan and your hands
12 cups popped corn (from about ⅓ cup raw kernels)
½ cup corn syrup (dark or light)
1 cup sugar
½ teaspoon salt
1 teaspoon vinegar (any type)
1 teaspoon pure vanilla extract

1. Preheat the oven to 250°F.

2. Brush a large roasting pan with some softened butter and add the popped corn. Place in the oven to warm while you prepare the syrup.

3. In a heavy-bottomed saucepan, combine 4 tablespoons butter, corn syrup, and sugar and bring to a boil, stirring constantly. Continue to boil the syrup for 2 more minutes, stirring. Very carefully remove from the heat and stir in the salt, vinegar, and vanilla. (Use extra caution, as the syrup will be very hot.)

4. Wearing oven mitts to protect your hands, carefully pour the syrup evenly over the warm popcorn in the roasting pan, mixing well with a wooden spoon to combine. When the mixture is cool enough to handle, butter your hands and form the mixture into 3-inch balls. Place them on a wire rack to cool completely before serving.

Eating in NEVA

Life was once rough in the Nevada desert, but electricity and refrigeration changed that. Once these modern conveniences arrived, the state filled with boomtowns. And the biggest boomtown of all is Las Vegas.

Today, this shining city in the desert draws roughly 40 million tourists every year from around the world. They come for the nightlife and endless casinos where gamblers hope to strike it rich. On the famous street called the Las Vegas Strip, you can watch acrobats, hear concerts, or visit replicas of New York's Coney Island, Paris's Eiffel Tower, and the canals of Venice. The food here is just as over the top. Many resorts and casinos feature round-the-clock, all-you-can-eat buffets, probably so gamblers will stay and keep sticking quarters in the slot machines!

Many of the world's most famous chefs have opened fine restaurants in Nevada. They fly in ingredients from far away, and then tempt guests with luxury foods such as towering sushi, Italian truffles, and rich desserts. Today, one casino sells an ice cream sundae that costs $1,000. It's covered in a thin layer of edible gold!

DA

ANTELOPE

Pronghorn antelope were once an essential food—so much so that they became an endangered species. Thanks to preservation efforts, Nevada is again a place where these antelope play.

SALTY LEMONADE

When the Hoover Dam was built in the 1930s, workers in the hot sun lost so much salt through their sweat that doctors required them to put lots of salt in their food and lemonade.

CARSON CITY ★

CAVIAR

Las Vegas features fancy cuisine in restaurants run by some of the best chefs in the world. Winning gamblers splurge on expensive foods including steak and caviar.

WILD ONION

Nevada is the driest state in America. One plant that thrives in this climate is a wild onion named after the state, *Allium nevadense*.

BIGHORN SHEEP

The state animal is the desert bighorn sheep, whose impressive curled horns can grow up to three feet long! Sheep meat has been a desert food source for thousands of years.

FRY BREAD

Fry bread is popular at Native American pow wows and Southwest state fairs, often as a "Navajo taco" topped with refried beans, lettuce, tomato, and shredded cheese.

Lamb Chops with Basque Seasoning

PREPARATION TIME	COOKING TIME	LEVEL OF DIFFICULTY	SERVES
15 minutes, plus overnight marinating time	8 minutes	● ● ○	4

During the Gold Rush of the mid–1800s, immigrants from the Basque region of Spain headed west in search of their fortunes; many became shepherds tending herds of sheep in the mountains. Today, you can still find Basque hotels and restaurants out in the Nevada countryside, serving lots of lamb alongside cabbage soup, garlicky mushrooms, and fried potatoes.

INGREDIENTS

8 lamb loin chops (about 2 pounds)
¼ cup plus 2 tablespoons extra-virgin olive oil
2 tablespoons fresh lemon juice
2 teaspoons Dijon mustard
3 garlic cloves, minced
2 teaspoons chopped fresh rosemary
1 teaspoon smoked sweet paprika (Spanish pimenton)
Coarse salt and freshly ground pepper

SPECIAL EQUIPMENT

a meat thermometer

1. In a bowl large enough to hold the chops, whisk to combine ¼ cup oil with the lemon juice, mustard, garlic, rosemary, and paprika. Add the lamb to the bowl and massage it with the marinade. Cover and marinate in the refrigerator 8–24 hours.

2. In a heavy skillet, heat remaining 2 tablespoons oil over medium-high heat. Pat chops dry and season with salt and pepper. Cook half the lamb until nicely browned on the bottom, about 4 minutes. Using tongs, flip and cook until the internal temperature reaches 125°F (for medium-rare meat), about 4 minutes longer.

3. Transfer the chops to a plate and tent with foil to keep warm. Add the remaining 4 chops and cook as directed. Transfer to another plate, tent with foil, and let chops rest for about 3 minutes before serving.

Eating in NEW HAMPSHIRE

New Hampshire's White Mountains draw visitors to ski in the long winters, hike among the wildflowers in the spring, jump into lakes all summer, and "peep" at the brightly colored leaves each autumn. These outdoor adventures can work up quite an appetite for the hearty fare that New Hampshire "Yankees" have been cooking for generations.

Sit down for dinner in New Hampshire and you can just taste that you're in the heart of New England. *Yankee* magazine is headquartered here, celebrating New England traditions. Locals like life the way it's been for centuries, and that's true for food, too. Family farms here still produce lots of wonderful maple syrup, apples, and dairy, and still cook Yankee classics: pot roast, salt cod cakes, baked beans, and squash soup. Breakfast might be an apple cider donut from a local orchard, dunked in a cup of creamy farm-fresh milk.

New Hampshire also has a tiny sliver of Atlantic coastline, so fresh seafood is always on the menu. Even up in the White Mountains, away from the ocean, people love lobster rolls and bowls of fish chowder.

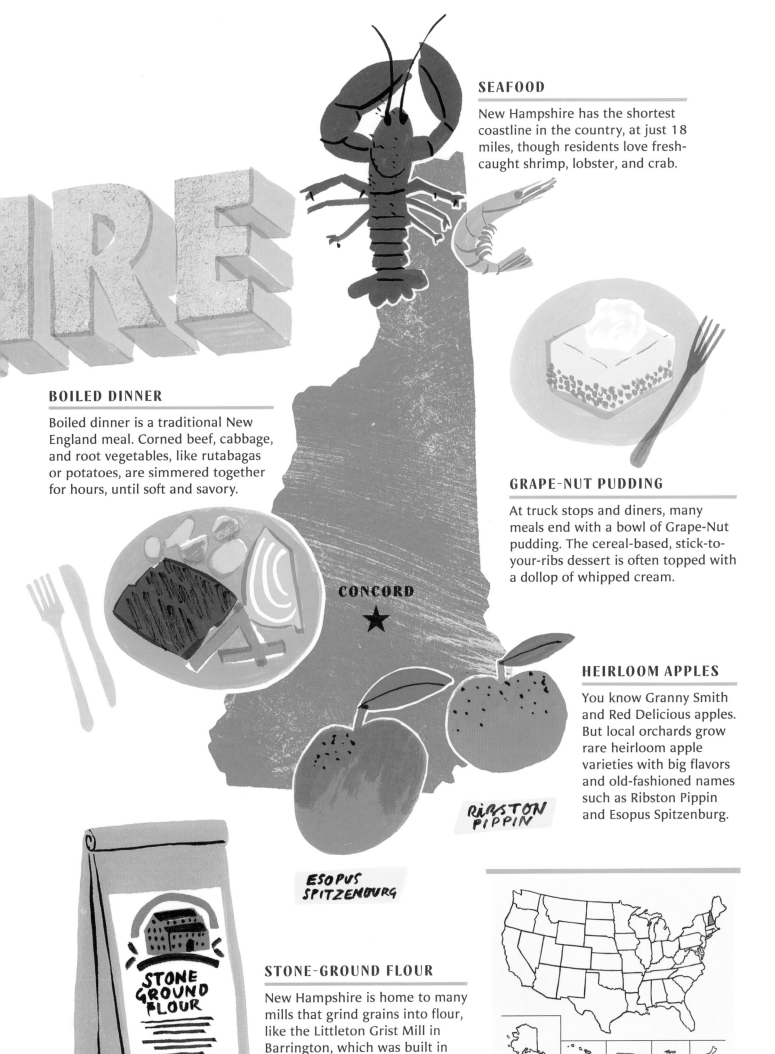

SEAFOOD

New Hampshire has the shortest coastline in the country, at just 18 miles, though residents love fresh-caught shrimp, lobster, and crab.

BOILED DINNER

Boiled dinner is a traditional New England meal. Corned beef, cabbage, and root vegetables, like rutabagas or potatoes, are simmered together for hours, until soft and savory.

GRAPE-NUT PUDDING

At truck stops and diners, many meals end with a bowl of Grape-Nut pudding. The cereal-based, stick-to-your-ribs dessert is often topped with a dollop of whipped cream.

CONCORD

HEIRLOOM APPLES

You know Granny Smith and Red Delicious apples. But local orchards grow rare heirloom apple varieties with big flavors and old-fashioned names such as Ribston Pippin and Esopus Spitzenburg.

RIBSTON PIPPIN

ESOPUS SPITZENBURG

STONE GROUND FLOUR

STONE-GROUND FLOUR

New Hampshire is home to many mills that grind grains into flour, like the Littleton Grist Mill in Barrington, which was built in 1798. Its buckwheat flour makes excellent pancakes.

Maple Custard

PREPARATION TIME	**COOKING TIME**	**LEVEL OF DIFFICULTY**	**SERVES**
15 minutes	45 minutes	● ● ○	6

New Hampshire's cold northern climate means that summer feels short and winter can feel very long. Folks here don't seem to mind, however—maybe because they can enjoy cozy desserts like this one year-round, sweetened with local maple syrup. The darker syrup has a stronger maple flavor. Look for "Dark Grade, Robust Flavor" on the label. Like many custards and cheesecakes, this recipe requires baking in a bath of boiling water, called a bain marie, to keep the texture silky smooth.

INGREDIENTS
2 cups heavy (whipping) cream
½ cup milk
½ cup pure maple syrup
2 tablespoons pure maple sugar
6 large egg yolks

SPECIAL EQUIPMENT
6 (6-oz) ramekins or custard cups, fine-mesh sieve

1. Preheat the oven to 325°F. Set a fine-mesh sieve over a medium bowl. Fill a kettle with several cups of water and bring to a boil.

2. In a medium saucepan, stir to combine the cream, milk, maple syrup, and maple sugar, and bring just to a simmer over medium-low heat. Do not allow to boil.

3. Meanwhile, in a large bowl, whisk the egg yolks. Whisk a ladle of the hot cream mixture into the yolks to warm them. Whisking constantly, pour the remaining hot cream into the warmed yolks. Strain the whole mixture through the sieve into the medium bowl.

4. Place six 6-ounce ramekins or custard cups in a baking pan. Dividing evenly, ladle the custard into the ramekins. Very carefully pour boiling water into the bottom of the pan to reach halfway up the cups, being careful not to pour any water into the cups. Cover the whole pan with a sheet of foil. Bake in the oven until the custard is just set (there should be a ¼-inch thick area in the center of each that is still loose), 35–40 minutes. Transfer the pan to a wire rack (the custard will fully set as it cools). Serve custard warm or chilled.

Eating in NEW JE[RSEY]

New Jersey is the most densely populated state, but despite the crowds, it's also famous for its fields of fresh fruits and vegetables. That's why it's known as the Garden State.

The reputation goes back a century, when New Jersey's farmers were busy growing produce to feed the millions of people living in New York City, just across the Hudson River. Daily trains delivered fresh crops of strawberries, blueberries, cranberries, corn, and tomatoes from the Garden State to the city streets of Manhattan. Today, people still look forward to summer harvests of "Jersey corn" and "Jersey tomatoes."

That's not the only way that New York City has influenced the foods of its next-door neighbor. As the Big Apple draws immigrants from around the world, New Jersey has become home to people—and cuisines—from across the globe. Today, one-fifth of Jersey residents are immigrants, including many from India, Mexico, Korea, and the Dominican Republic. So, you can enjoy their foods in New Jersey any night of the week!

The Garden State is also home to 1.5 million Italian-Americans. They love cooking spaghetti sauce and lasagna using those famous Jersey tomatoes!

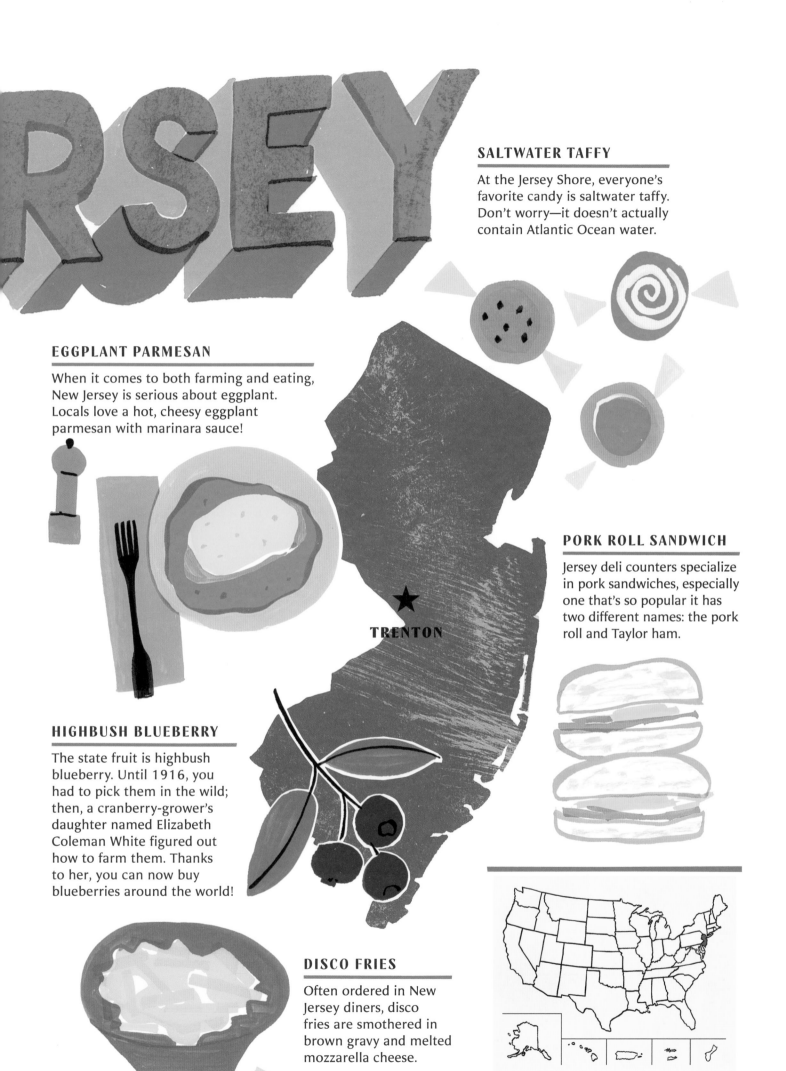

RSEY

SALTWATER TAFFY

At the Jersey Shore, everyone's favorite candy is saltwater taffy. Don't worry—it doesn't actually contain Atlantic Ocean water.

EGGPLANT PARMESAN

When it comes to both farming and eating, New Jersey is serious about eggplant. Locals love a hot, cheesy eggplant parmesan with marinara sauce!

PORK ROLL SANDWICH

Jersey deli counters specialize in pork sandwiches, especially one that's so popular it has two different names: the pork roll and Taylor ham.

HIGHBUSH BLUEBERRY

The state fruit is highbush blueberry. Until 1916, you had to pick them in the wild; then, a cranberry-grower's daughter named Elizabeth Coleman White figured out how to farm them. Thanks to her, you can now buy blueberries around the world!

TRENTON

DISCO FRIES

Often ordered in New Jersey diners, disco fries are smothered in brown gravy and melted mozzarella cheese.

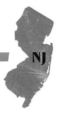

Bacon, Lettuce, and Tomato (BLT) Sandwich

PREPARATION TIME	COOKING TIME	LEVEL OF DIFFICULTY	SERVES
5 minutes	10 minutes	● ○ ○	1

In New Jersey, sandwiches are big—literally. People here make them bigger, and better, than just about anywhere else. Summers in New Jersey mean fresh beefsteak tomatoes, sold by the truckload at roadside stands and farmers' markets. The BLT is a summer classic, but New Jerseyans also famously love the tomato sandwich with nothing more than mayonnaise and salt—essentially a BLT without the B and the L.

INGREDIENTS
2 or 3 slices thick-cut bacon
2 slices sandwich bread
¼ cup mayonnaise
Lettuce (romaine, iceberg,
   or whatever else you like)
1 ripe, juicy beefsteak
   tomato, sliced thick
Freshly ground black pepper
   (optional)

1. In a skillet, cook bacon over medium heat until brown and crisp, flipping occasionally. Transfer to a paper towel-lined plate to drain.

2. Toast bread, then generously spread one side of each slice with mayonnaise. Layer bacon, lettuce, and tomato over mayonnaise on one slice. Season with a few grinds of black pepper, if desired, then top with other slice of bread, mayonnaise-side down. Slice sandwich in half, and serve.

Eating in NEW MEX

While summers in New Mexico are hot, it's the chile peppers that have locals really sweating. For centuries, Natives have grown chile peppers in the land now known as New Mexico. People here grow hundreds of types, sized from smaller than your pinky to bigger than your hand, and from mild or fruity to make-you-cry hot.

People often think of peppers by color. Green chiles are harvested young, then roasted and blended into sauces. If left on the plant longer, the green peppers ripen to a bright red. You'll see these dried to a crimson crisp and hanging on strings in the markets of Santa Fe. When it's time to cook, people grind them into a delicious, spicy red sauce.

All these peppers spice up New Mexican recipes: they're simmered into soups, baked into cornbread, stirred into salsas, stuffed into chiles rellenos, enchiladas, and tamales, and served at breakfast in huevos rancheros (that's Spanish for "ranch-style eggs"). Every September, a festival celebrates New Mexico's green chiles in Hatch Valley, known as the "Chile Capital of the World."

CHILE PEPPERS

The state's official question ("Red or green?") refers to chile peppers. When ordering red and green together, diners just say "Christmas!"

PIÑON NUTS

Native Americans still harvest delicious piñon nuts from the cones of wild pine trees. Some are baked into piñon cakes.

POSOLE

Hominy (giant, dried corn kernels) are simmered with green chiles and shredded pork or chicken. Bowls of this hearty stew are often topped with sliced radishes and fried tortilla strips.

SANTA FE
★

CARNE ADOVADA

Carne adovada (Spanish for "marinated meat") is pork cooked in red chile sauce with vinegar. The tender meat is served with corn tortillas.

SPICY PIE

New Mexican apple pie is baked with spicy Hatch chiles and often eaten with a scoop of vanilla—the ice cream cools the heat!

PRICKLY PEAR CACTUS

The sweet fruit of the prickly pear is used in jams and jellies, and the green pads, called nopales, are delicious in salads or tacos.

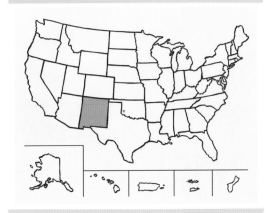

Biscochitos

PREPARATION TIME	COOKING TIME	LEVEL OF DIFFICULTY	MAKES
25 minutes, plus 30 minutes chilling time	50 minutes	● ● ○	36–48 cookies

The official state cookies of New Mexico, these nicely spiced, shortbread-like bites are especially popular at Christmas, served with hot chocolate. They are traditionally made with lard (pork fat), but vegetable shortening makes a fine substitute. Crushing the anise seed helps to release the flavor.

INGREDIENTS

3 cups all-purpose flour, plus more for work surface
1½ teaspoons baking powder
1 tablespoon anise seed, lightly crushed with a mortar and pestle or the bottom of a heavy skillet
½ teaspoon salt
1¼ cups lard or vegetable shortening
2¾ cups sugar
1 teaspoon pure vanilla extract
1 large egg
2 teaspoons ground cinnamon

SPECIAL EQUIPMENT

a 2-inch round cookie cutter

1. In a large bowl, whisk to combine the flour, baking powder, anise seed, and salt.

2. In another large bowl, beat the lard and ¾ cup of the sugar with an electric mixer until light and fluffy, about 4 minutes. Beat in the vanilla and egg. On low speed, gradually beat in the flour mixture. Cover with plastic wrap and refrigerate for 30 minutes.

3. Position a rack in the middle of the oven and preheat to 350°F. Line a baking sheet with parchment paper.

4. In another large bowl, whisk to combine the remaining 2 cups sugar and the cinnamon, and set aside.

5. Lightly flour a work surface, and place dough on it. Roll dough to a rectangle ¼-inch thick. Using the cutter, cut out cookies and place ½ inch apart on the lined baking sheet. Bake until just set, 10–12 minutes. Let the cookies cool for 1 minute on the sheet, then place a few at a time into the large bowl of cinnamon sugar. Working quickly, toss very gently to cover the warm cookies with the mixture. Transfer to a wire rack to cool completely.

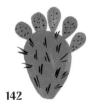

Eating in NEW YO

New York State is mostly beautiful farmland, including dairies, orchards, and more fields of cabbage than any other state. But when you say "New York," few people think of cabbage. They think of New York City!

Down in the southeast corner of this state stands the biggest city in America. New York, New York ("the town so nice, they named it twice!") isn't the capital of the United States. It isn't even the capital of New York State! (That's Albany, upstate.) But it *is* an unofficial capital of the world, drawing immigrants from near and far. And that means you can taste flavors from just about anywhere, simply by hopping on the subway.

At the United Nations, in Manhattan, representatives meet from 193 nations—which is about how many cuisines you can try in this city! New York may be famous for bagels, pizza, and cheesecake. But you can also order Russian borscht, Senegalese stew, Afghani kebabs, Brazilian black beans, Nepalese dumplings, Colombian arepas, and Syrian pita breads—just to name a few!

An old song about New York promises that if you can make it here, you'll make it anywhere. But you could also sing, about foods of the world, "if they make it anywhere, they make it here!"

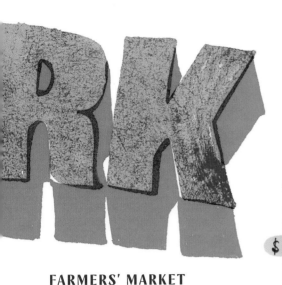

CONCORD GRAPES

Sweet Concord grapes grow in the Lake Erie region. They are pressed into grape juice or turned into grape jelly, but the best way to enjoy this fall fruit is in a Concord grape pie.

APPLES

The city may be known as the Big Apple, but apple-orchard country is upstate. Farm stands sell sweet cider, cider donuts, and about 100 different varieties of apples.

FARMERS' MARKET

New York City is home to one of the largest networks of farmers' markets in the country. The largest is at Union Square, where thousands of New Yorkers (including hundreds of chefs) buy fresh farm foods year-round.

QUEENS

Queens is the most ethnically diverse of New York City's five boroughs, with nearly half its residents born outside the US. You can get food from Burma, Colombia, Ecuador, Taiwan, India, Poland, Korea, Haiti, and just about anywhere else on Earth.

ALBANY

LATIN FLAVORS

Dominican immigrants brought tres leches cakes, green plantain mangu, tostones, and a cold, creamy orange drink called *morir soñando*, which means "to die dreaming."

LONG ISLAND SEAFOOD

Hudson River oysters were once so abundant that one writer nicknamed New York City "the Big Oyster." These days, fresh seafood comes in from Long Island.

BAGELS AND LOX

New York City has the world's second-largest Jewish population, but its Jewish delis are second to none. Specialties include rye bread, challah, bagels with lox, pastrami sandwiches, and kosher dill pickles.

HOT DOGS

Historians say hot dogs, descended from German frankfurters, first appeared on Brooklyn's Coney Island boardwalk. A restaurant called Nathan's Famous still holds a hot dog eating contest there every Fourth of July.

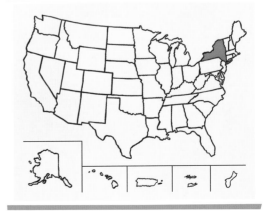

Quick-Pickled Cucumbers

PREPARATION TIME	LEVEL OF DIFFICULTY	MAKES
15 minutes, plus overnight pickling	● ○ ○	2 quarts

In the 1800s, there were so many pickle barrels and pushcarts in New York City that maybe it should've been called the Big Pickle instead of the Big Apple. Pickling has recently become popular in the city again, especially in Brooklyn, where farm-to-table cooks preserve cucumbers and other vegetables grown in community gardens and on city rooftops. Unlike fermented pickles, which require a few weeks before they're ready to eat, these quick pickles can be enjoyed just one day after you prepare them.

INGREDIENTS

1½ pounds Kirby or other small cucumbers, halved or quartered lengthwise
3 tablespoons coarse salt
2 tablespoons sugar
1¼ cups distilled white vinegar
1 tablespoon coriander seeds
1 tablespoon yellow mustard seeds
2 teaspoons black peppercorns

1. Pack the cucumbers into 2 clean, sealable 1-quart glass jars or plastic containers.

2. In another container, make the brine by combining the remaining ingredients. Close the container and shake well until the salt and sugar dissolve.

3. Pour the brine over the cucumbers, dividing evenly between the two jars. Add just enough room temperature water to each jar to cover the cucumbers. Close the jars and turn over and back once to mix the brine with the water. Refrigerate overnight or for up to 3 weeks.

Eating in NORTH CAROLINA

In North Carolina, "barbecue" doesn't mean burgers on a grill. It means giant pieces of pork, cooked for hours over hardwood until it's perfumed with smoke, and so tender it's falling apart.

North Carolina is home to not one but *two* of America's great styles of barbecue, and people feel very strongly about the right way to cook it. In the eastern part of the state, cooks go "whole hog," smoking an entire pig for hours and seasoning it with a vinegar-pepper sauce. At the other end of the state, the town of Lexington (home to more than twenty barbecue joints!) is headquarters of the western style, cooking just the pork shoulder and sweetening the sauce with tomato. Barbecue chefs, called pit masters, spend years perfecting techniques. Some cook their 'cue in underground pits, while others cook in special metal smokers called "rigs," which can be as big as a car. And whether you eat your barbecue with a knife and fork, or tucked into a squishy bun, don't forget to order coleslaw and fried cornmeal "hush puppies" on the side.

People in North Carolina love to argue over which kind of barbecue is better. But here's something they can all agree on: the best kind of party is a big, messy pig pickin'. Bring napkins!

SCUPPERNONG GRAPES

Huge, sweet scuppernong grapes are the state fruit. The famous "Mother Vine" is said to be more than 400 years old, and is believed to be the oldest cultivated grapevine in the US.

PIMIENTO CHEESE

Pimiento cheese is a mixture of grated cheddar, mayonnaise, and chopped pimiento peppers. People spread it on white bread for one of the most popular sandwiches in the South.

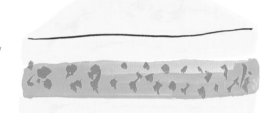

RALEIGH

MORAVIAN SUGAR CAKES

The Moravian Church of Winston-Salem is famous for its sweet sugar cakes, served every Easter.

TAR HEEL PIE

Tar heel pie looks as if it might contain tar, but it's actually gooey chocolate with pecans.

HOPPIN' JOHN

Hoppin' John is a mix of black-eyed peas and rice. Eating it on New Year's Day is said to bring good luck.

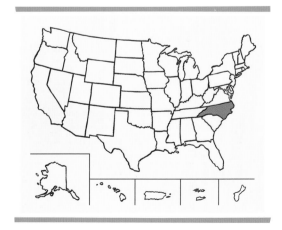

Slow-Cooker Pork Shoulder

PREPARATION TIME	COOKING TIME	LEVEL OF DIFFICULTY	SERVES
10 minutes	8 hours	● ● ○	10–12

Hold the logs and matches! While real Carolina pit masters smoke their meat over wood, this is an easy indoor version. And the rich, thick, tomato-based sauce captures the famous flavors of Lexington barbecue. The sauce soaks into the smoky, succulent meat for a sweeter flavor than the tangy barbecue of eastern North Carolina. You'll be the star of any picnic with this dish, which makes plenty to share.

INGREDIENTS

For the sauce:
2 cups cider vinegar
½ cup ketchup
¼ cup packed dark brown sugar
2 tablespoons granulated sugar
1 tablespoon coarse salt
1 tablespoon ground white pepper
1 to 2 teaspoons crushed chili flakes (optional)
1 teaspoon freshly ground black pepper

For the pork:
1 tablespoon coarse salt
Freshly ground black pepper
5–6 pounds boneless pork shoulder, trimmed of all but ¼-inch fat (you can ask a butcher to do this for you)
½ cup chicken broth, preferably low-sodium
Rolls, coleslaw, and pickles for serving

SPECIAL EQUIPMENT
slow cooker (4-quart or bigger), fine-mesh sieve

1. Make the sauce: In a large bowl, whisk to combine vinegar, ketchup, both sugars, salt, white pepper, chili flakes, and black pepper. Measure out 1 cup and set aside, for cooking the pork. (The rest can be served with the meal, or stored in the refrigerator for up to 1 month.)

2. Make the pork: Pat pork dry and sprinkle well on all sides with the salt and ground pepper to taste. Nestle the pork in the slow cooker. Add the reserved 1 cup sauce and the chicken broth to the cooker, turning pork over until it's coated. Cover slow cooker and cook on low until pork is tender enough to pull apart with a fork, about 8 hours.

3. Using tongs, lift the pork and transfer to a baking sheet. When it's cool enough to handle, use 2 forks to pull pork into shreds.

4. Set a fine-mesh sieve over a large saucepan. Strain the cooking liquid from the slow cooker into the saucepan and bring to a boil over high heat. Boil until the liquid is thickened, 5 to 10 minutes. Add the pulled pork to the saucepan and stir until heated through. Serve with rolls, coleslaw, pickles, and additional sauce, if desired.

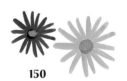

Eating in NORTH DAKOTA

The cold dry climate of the Great Plains is perfect for wheat. But to rotate crops, farmers in the Red River Valley began planting a sweet root crop as well: sugar beets. These beets aren't eaten as a vegetable. Instead they're turned into an alternative to cane sugar. The big beet harvest brought Germans and Russians to work the fields, and they brought along their favorite foods, many of which are still popular here, like plum cakes, rib-sticking creamy stews, and hearty potato dumplings. Later, Mexican workers known as *betabeleros* came to join the beet harvest. Thanks to them, North Dakota kitchens now cook tasty pinto beans and tortillas, too.

Sugar beets aren't the only reason North Dakota is sweet. The state is covered with huge fields of native grasses, as well as big crops of sunflowers, clover, and alfalfa, all of which attract honey bees! Bees love it here so much that North Dakota produces more honey than any other state in the nation!

To really sample North Dakota sweetness, visit the town of Fargo and ask for Carol Widman's Candy Co. For more than a century, they've candied North Dakota's best-known crops. Try the chocolate-covered wheat berries, soybeans, potato chips, or sunflower seeds. Sweet!

CHOKECHERRIES

The bright red chokecherry was used by Great Plains Indians as medicine and in tea. In 2007, an elementary school class wrote to the state government suggesting they make chokecherry the official fruit. It worked!

HONEYBEE

North Dakota's bees are busy! They make about 34 million pounds of honey a year — more than any other state.

WINTER SQUASH

The Lewis and Clark expedition passed through present-day North Dakota as it traveled up the Missouri River. The explorers spent the winter with the Mandan people, known for expertly growing corn, squash, and sunflowers.

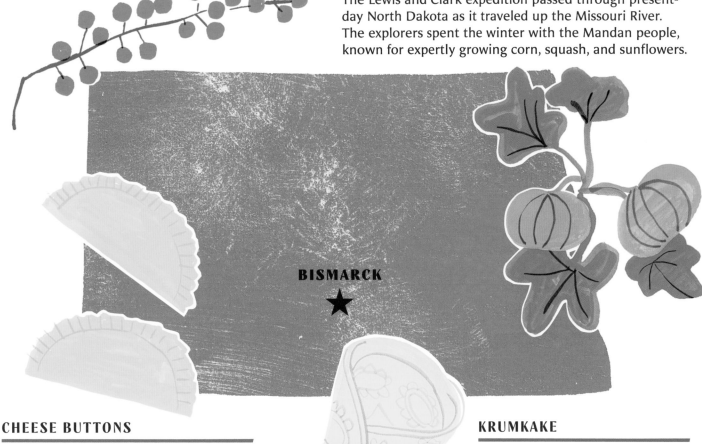

BISMARCK

CHEESE BUTTONS

In the 19th and early 20th centuries, immigrants from Germany and Russia settled here in sod houses. These days, their great-great-grandchildren still make "cheese buttons," or dough stuffed with cottage cheese, then boiled or fried.

KRUMKAKE

Swedish immigrants brought *krumkake* cookies to North Dakota. The crisp little waffles are rolled up into cones and sometimes filled with whipped cream.

CANOLA FLOWERS

Fields of bright yellow canola flowers bloom across the state. Canola is related to broccoli but farmed for its seeds, which are made into oils for baking, cooking, and frying.

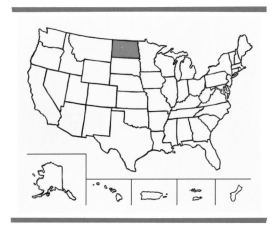

Smashed Jerusalem Artichokes

PREPARATION TIME	COOKING TIME	LEVEL OF DIFFICULTY	SERVES
10 minutes	40 minutes	● ● ○	4–6

Jerusalem artichokes are starchy tubers that are not related to artichokes at all. They are also known as sunchokes because they grow in the roots of giant sunflowers. The towering, flowering plants grow wild in the Great Plains and beyond, thriving especially well in North Dakota. Sliced raw, the crisp tubers taste nutty and sweet. Once cooked, the texture is similar to that of a potato. Look for them at farmers' markets and supermarkets from mid-fall to spring.

INGREDIENTS

1 pound Jerusalem artichokes, scrubbed
2 tablespoons extra-virgin olive oil, plus more for drizzling
Coarse salt and freshly ground pepper
1 tablespoon chopped fresh thyme or rosemary

1. Preheat the oven to 400°F. Line a baking sheet with parchment paper.

2. Toss artichokes with 2 tablespoons olive oil on the baking sheet, and season with salt and pepper. Place baking sheet in oven, and roast until artichokes are tender when pierced with a fork, 30 to 40 minutes, flipping them over halfway through.

3. Remove the baking sheet from the oven, and increase oven temperature to 450°F. Using a spatula or a heatproof plate, lightly press down on the artichokes so they are slightly flattened but still thick, with a little flesh coming out of the skins.

4. Lightly drizzle artichokes with oil and sprinkle with half the thyme or rosemary. Put them back into the oven and roast until crisp on the bottom, about 5 minutes. Flip each one and roast until crisp on other side, about 5 minutes more. Sprinkle with the remaining herbs, and serve.

Eating in OHIO

In the Buckeye State, people from cities and farms come together over dessert.

If you get invited to a wedding in Youngstown, don't expect cake. There, brides ask friends to bake for their "cookie table." Guests choose from hundreds of Italian butterballs, *pizzelles*, mini tarts, and kolache nut loaves.

Butler County is home to Ohio's twelve-stop "Donut Trail." Look for cheesecake donuts and pineapple fritters.

The Shakers, a religious community that lived in Ohio for many years, cooked for such big groups that they perfected the apple peeler and the cherry pitter to speed up their from-scratch pie making. Shaker Lemon Pie, also known as Ohio Lemon Pie, features lemons sliced paper-thin, peel and all, baked into the filling.

Ohio is also famous for ice cream. Creameries throughout the state churn local cream into frozen pints. Jeni's Splendid Ice Cream in Columbus turns Ohio ingredients into special seasonal flavors that include lavender, popcorn, blackberry, and backyard mint.

CHICKEN PAPRIKASH

Hungarian immigrants introduced their new Cleveland neighbors to a recipe called chicken paprikash. It's flavored with the sweet red pepper powder known as paprika.

PAWPAW FRUIT

The pawpaw is the largest tree fruit that grows in America, with a custard-like texture and a tropical taste. Southern Ohio has some of the best pawpaw patches anywhere. The state made pawpaw its official native fruit and hosts a pawpaw festival each September.

GOETTA

ITALIAN

BRATWURST

APPLES

The real-life Johnny Appleseed planted apple orchards across Ohio in the 1800s. Today, you can visit the Johnny Appleseed Museum in Urbana!

SPACE FOOD

PANCAKES & BACON

COLUMBUS

ASTRONAUT FOOD

More astronauts have come from Ohio than from any other state. When in outer space, they survive on dry food and semiliquids squeezed out of a tube.

POLISH SAUSAGES

Ohio is home to all kinds of wursts (sausages) brought by European immigrants. Today, you can find the Polish Boy sandwich, bratwurst, Italian sausages, and *goetta* —a meat-and-oat sausage eaten for breakfast!

SKYLINE CHILI

In Cincinnati, skyline chili is seasoned with chocolate and cinnamon, served on spaghetti, and topped with a mound of shredded cheese. Add onions and beans to make it a "five-way"!

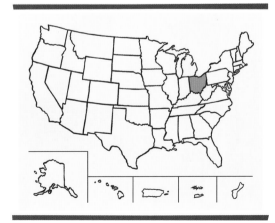

Buckeye Candies

PREPARATION TIME	COOKING TIME	LEVEL OF DIFFICULTY	MAKES
1 hour, plus 30 minutes chilling time	5 minutes	● ● ○	72

This homemade candy is served at just about every gathering in the Buckeye State, including Ohio State football games. The peanut butter fudge is dipped in melted chocolate just enough to leave a little circle of peanut butter peeking out, so it looks like a horse chestnut, or "buckeye."

INGREDIENTS

2 cups smooth peanut butter
4 tablespoons unsalted butter, room temperature
1 teaspoon salt
3¾ cups powdered sugar
1 (12-ounce) bag semisweet chocolate chips (2 cups)
2 tablespoons solid vegetable shortening

1. Line a tray with waxed paper or parchment. In a large bowl, with an electric mixer, cream the peanut butter, butter, and salt until the butter is thoroughly incorporated, about 2 minutes.

2. On low speed, gradually beat in the powdered sugar, then increase to medium speed and beat until smooth, about 3 minutes.

3. Use your hands to shape the mixture into 1-inch balls. Place them on the tray, and refrigerate until firm, as little as 30 minutes or as long as overnight.

4. Fill a saucepan with an inch or two of water, and bring to a simmer. In a heatproof bowl set over the simmering water, melt the chocolate chips and shortening until smooth. Using a toothpick, dip each peanut butter ball into the chocolate, leaving the top of each ball uncovered so that it resembles a buckeye, and transfer back to the lined tray.

5. After they have all been dipped, smooth over the holes left by the toothpick. Refrigerate, covered, until ready to serve, up to 1 week.

Eating in OKLAH...

"*Oh, what a beautiful morning, oh what a beautiful day, I've got a beautiful feeling, everything's going my way!*"

So begins the musical "Oklahoma," celebrating frontier life in 1906. But back in 1830, this state wasn't yet home to cowboys. It wasn't even called Oklahoma! It was Indian Territory. Under President Jackson, the US government sent native people here. By 1840, nearly 100,000 Cherokee, Seminole, Creek, Choctaw, and Chickasaw people had walked here on a terrible journey called the "Trail of Tears." The Natives made new homes and tried new foods, including local berries, fish, and game. And the place got a new name: Oklahoma, which means "Land of the Red Man" in Choctaw.

Over time Oklahoma became home to lots of frontier settlers— the type who inspired the musical. In the show, cowboys bid on lunches cooked by their sweethearts, complete with meat pies, apple jelly, and "sweet pertater pie."

If you visit Oklahoma, you can sample native foods like bison. Or enjoy the official state meal, a gut-busting menu that includes fried okra, cornbread, barbecue pork, chicken-fried steak, black-eyed peas, and pecan pie. It might inspire you to break into song.

SAND PLUM JELLY

Oklahomans simmer wild sand plums into a golden-red jelly.

EASTERN REDBUD

The state tree, called the Eastern Redbud, has pretty, purple-pink blossoms that are edible. Locals toss them over salads and even ice cream.

ICED TEA

Like many Southerners, people in Oklahoma keep cool with iced tea. Ask for "unsweet," or get a glass as sweet as soda.

★ **OKLAHOMA CITY**

OKLAHOMA "PRIME RIB"

Barbecue joints offer Oklahoma "prime rib." It's bologna, slow-smoked until the skin is bronzed, then served sliced or in sandwiches topped with barbecue sauce.

PECAN PIE

Pecan pie is big in Oklahoma, its gooey center filled with the state's own pecan crop.

ONION-FRIED BURGER

This burger has thinly sliced onions cooked right into the patty. It's so popular in the city of El Reno that if you simply order a burger, it's what you'll get.

CRAPPIES

Oklahomans love to go fishing in the state's freshwater lakes and streams. Fish called crappies are especially popular with those who like to "hook 'em and cook 'em."

161

Chicken-Fried Steak

PREPARATION TIME	COOKING TIME	LEVEL OF DIFFICULTY	SERVES
15 minutes	20 minutes	●●●	4

Despite its name, this delicious dinner doesn't actually contain any chicken. Instead, a tough cut of steak is pounded thin to make it tender; then it's coated (dredged) in flour and fried like chicken, hence the name. Hot from the frying pan, the crispy, battered steak is served with creamy white gravy seasoned with black pepper, alongside mashed potatoes, green beans, or sweet corn. Many restaurants deep-fry the steaks, but it's easier to shallow-fry in a home kitchen.

INGREDIENTS

1¼ cups all-purpose flour
Coarse salt and freshly
ground black pepper
2 large eggs
1 pound beef top round, cut
crosswise into 4 slices
½ cup vegetable oil
2 cups milk, plus more if
needed

SPECIAL EQUIPMENT

meat mallet or rolling pin

1. Preheat the oven to 250°F. Place a wire rack on a large rimmed baking sheet and place near the oven.

2. Set up a dredging station: In a wide shallow bowl, season 1 cup flour generously with salt and pepper. In a second shallow bowl, lightly beat the eggs. Line a baking sheet with wax or parchment paper.

3. Place the beef between sheets of plastic wrap on a sturdy work surface. Using a meat mallet or rolling pin, pound the meat into steaks ¼-inch thick. Dip the steaks in the seasoned flour to cover completely, then in the eggs, and then back in the flour, covering completely and shaking off any excess. Place on the lined baking sheet until ready to fry. Keep the bowl of seasoned flour handy (the steaks will be dredged again).

4. Add the oil to a large (12-inch) cast-iron skillet (or other large heavy high-sided frying pan) and heat until just starting to shimmer.

5. Meanwhile, dip steaks, one at a time, back in the seasoned flour. Working in batches of 2, fry the steaks until the coating is crisp and golden brown, about 3 minutes per side. Transfer the cooked steaks to the wire rack and place the baking sheet in the oven while you prepare the gravy.

6. Carefully spoon off and discard some of the fat, leaving a shallow coating in the skillet. Add the remaining ¼ cup flour to the fat in the pan and cook, whisking constantly, until the paste darkens to a golden brown, about 3 minutes.

7. Gradually whisk in the milk and bring to a boil. If you prefer thinner gravy, whisk in a little more milk. Season the gravy with salt and pepper. Serve steaks with the gravy spooned on top.

Eating in OREGON

In Oregon, people dive to the ocean floor and hike to the mountaintops, all in pursuit of delicious Northwest flavors.

On the Pacific coast, people catch shrimp and halibut. They go clamming or set crab pots. In Oregon's rivers, salmon swim upstream to spawn. You can fish for trout—or go white-water rafting—on the Rogue River. Hiking the Coast Range forest, you can gather curled fiddlehead ferns in spring and golden chanterelle mushrooms in fall. Farther east, in the Willamette Valley's gentle climate, families pick wild berries to dry, freeze, or make into jam.

The towering, snow-capped Cascade Mountains are full of fishing lakes and hiking trails. The valleys grow bountiful fruit orchards. Oregonians go to an area called the Fruit Loop to pick apricots and peaches in summer, and then pears and apples in fall.

And in Oregon's largest city, Portland, inventive chefs combine all these special Northwest ingredients into spectacular menus that draw food-loving tourists from around the world.

MARIONBERRIES

Scientists at Oregon State University developed delicious new berry varieties that include marionberries and tayberries.

DUNGENESS CRAB

Oregonians eat lots of Dungeness crab cooked into soups, crab cakes, and even mac and cheese.

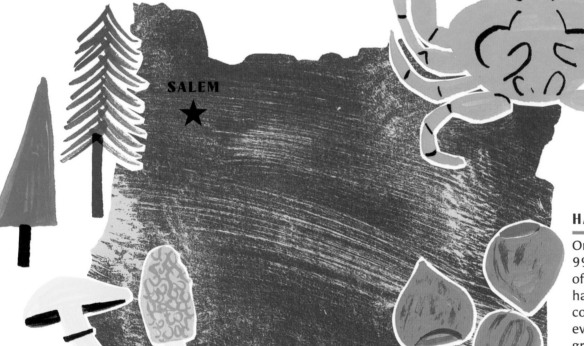

SALEM
★

HAZELNUTS

Oregon grows 99 percent of America's hazelnuts. People cook them into everything from granola to cookies to toppings for fruit crisp.

WILD MUSHROOMS

Oregon's coastal forests are rainy year-round, making them perfect spots for wild mushrooms such as chanterelles, matsutakes, and morels.

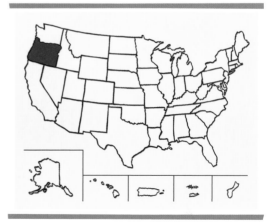

JAM-TOPPED SCONE

At the Oregon State Fair, you can enjoy a buttery, pillowy scone slathered with berry jam.

Granola with Hazelnuts and Cherries

PREPARATION TIME	COOKING TIME	LEVEL OF DIFFICULTY	MAKES
5 minutes	50 minutes	● ○ ○	about 12 cups

Easy to make and even easier to eat, granola is endlessly customizable. This version features two ingredients that grow well in the Beaver State— hazelnuts and cherries—but you can experiment by adding your favorite nuts, seeds, or dried fruits. Enjoy it by the bowlful with milk or yogurt, or do what Oregonians do: bring it along on the trail when you're out for a hike.

INGREDIENTS
½ cup honey
1 stick unsalted butter, melted
½ teaspoon ground cardamom
½ teaspoon ground cinnamon
¼ teaspoon salt
6 cups rolled oats
2 cups hazelnuts
1 cup unsweetened coconut flakes
½ cup hulled pumpkin seeds
2 cups dried cherries

1. Preheat the oven to 275°F. Line a rimmed baking sheet with foil.

2. In a large bowl, whisk together the honey, butter, cardamom, cinnamon, and salt until well combined. Add the oats, hazelnuts, coconut, and pumpkin seeds and mix with a flexible spatula to coat well.

3. Spread in a single layer on the baking sheet. Bake, stirring every 15 minutes, until medium-golden brown, 45–50 minutes. The granola will feel soft when you remove it from the oven, but will crisp up as it sits. Let cool completely, and then fold in the cherries. Granola can be stored in an airtight container at room temperature up to 2 weeks.

Eating in PENNSY

The old-fashioned "Pennsylvania Dutch" aren't Dutch at all. They were originally *Deutsch*—which means "German"—but over time some neighbors mistakenly called them Dutch, and it stuck. Despite the name, their descendants have kept their traditional German language, culture, and foods for more than 200 years, and tourists come to experience it all!

Visiting Pennsylvania Dutch towns is like going back in time. Many farming families choose to live without modern technology, and their foods can feel like time travel, too! At restaurants, you'll see women in bonnets serving meals such as chicken potpie, ham loaf, egg noodles, and *schnitz un knepp,* or pork with dried apples. Look for hard-boiled eggs pickled with beets that turn them bright pink! A hot pepper called a *hinkelhatz* (which means "chicken heart") is used in sauerkraut, which locals make from homegrown cabbage.

But it's not all meat and vegetables. The Pennsylvania Dutch make great sweets, too. In summer you might start a meal with a refreshingly cold fruit soup. Apple butter is sweet on home-baked bread. Famous local desserts include funnel cakes, apple dumplings, and shoofly pie.

LVANIA

BUTTON MUSHROOMS

The tiny town of Kennett Square, home to only six thousand people, grows more than a million pounds of mushrooms each week! That's half of all the mushrooms farmed in America.

CHOW CHOW

The Pennsylvania Dutch in Lancaster County are famous for their pretzels, apple butter, chow chow (a pickled vegetable salad), and molasses-based shoofly pies.

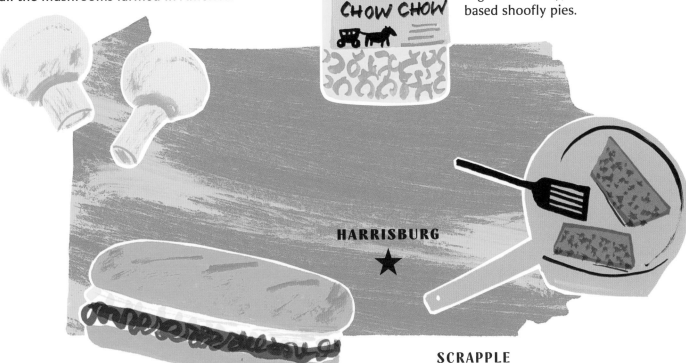

HARRISBURG ★

CHEESE STEAK

Philadelphians share the brotherly love of sandwiches. Cheese steaks, hoagies (the local nickname for subs), and Italian pork roast sandwiches were all invented in Pennsylvania's biggest city.

SCRAPPLE

Scrapple is a sausage-like dish of ground pork with cornmeal. Pennsylvanians fry up slices for breakfast.

PEPPER POT

In Philadelphia, you can still taste this beef tripe stew with lots of black pepper. Historians say the recipe got George Washington's soldiers through the terrible winter of 1778 and helped Americans win the Revolutionary War.

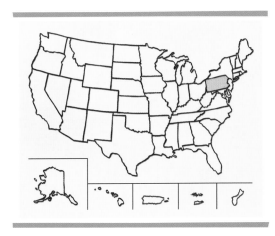

Soft Pretzels

PREPARATION TIME	COOKING TIME	LEVEL OF DIFFICULTY	MAKES
30 minutes, plus rising time	1 hour, 50 minutes	● ● ●	8 large pretzels

German immigrants introduced pretzels to Pennsylvania. Today, the state produces more pretzels than any other, often skillfully hand-formed by Amish women who can roll the fresh dough into just the right shape with a quick flick of the wrist.

INGREDIENTS
2 teaspoons active dry yeast
1 cup warm water (110°F)
2 tablespoons granulated sugar
1½ teaspoons salt
2½–3 cups all-purpose flour
¼ cup baking soda
1 tablespoon dark brown sugar
1 large egg
Coarse salt, for sprinkling
Vegetable oil, for bowl

1. In a large bowl, sprinkle the yeast over the water and let sit for 5 minutes. Stir in the sugar, salt, and 2 cups of the flour. Stir well. Add another ½ cup flour.

2. Lightly flour a work surface, and turn out the dough onto it. Knead the dough for 5–8 minutes, adding more flour if necessary, to make a smooth, soft, slightly tacky dough. Brush a large bowl with oil, and add the dough to it, turning it to coat completely. Cover with a damp kitchen towel and let the dough rise in a warm draft-free area until doubled in volume, about 1 hour.

3. Divide the dough evenly into 8 pieces. On work surface, roll each piece into a rope about 20 inches long. Form a pretzel shape by first forming a U shape, then bringing the arms of the U down and crossing them, twisting the cross and pressing the ends over the bottom of the U. Pinch the ends to seal. Place the pretzels on parchment-lined baking sheets, cover with a damp kitchen towel, and let rise for 20–30 minutes.

4. Preheat the oven to 425°F.

5. In a large, wide pot, combine 2 quarts water, baking soda, and brown sugar and bring to a boil. Reduce to a simmer. Using a skimmer or a slotted spoon, and working in batches if necessary (so as not to crowd the pot), lower the pretzels one at a time into the simmering water. Cook for 2 minutes, then flip over with the slotted spoon and cook 2 more minutes (you want to make sure each pretzel is boiled on both sides). Remove the pretzels and place them on the baking sheets.

6. Whisk the egg with 1 tablespoon warm water. Brush the pretzels with the egg wash and sprinkle with coarse salt. Bake until dark golden brown, 12–15 minutes. Transfer to wire racks to cool.

Eating in PUERTO

Puerto Rico, a territory of the United States, is known for its white sand beaches, clear blue water, and singing tree frogs. Its cuisine is famous, too, seasoned by three influences: native, Spanish, and West African. The native Taino and Arawak peoples grew cassava, hot peppers, corn, beans, and squash. The Spanish brought chicken, pork, goats, olive oil, and new spices to the Caribbean island. West Africans introduced bananas, coconuts, and coffee.

Puerto Rican menus today reflect these influences: dinner may be cassava root, fried and served with chicken or goat with spicy chorizo. And no matter what you eat, it's probably extra delicious thanks to *sofrito*, a mix of peppers, onions, garlic, chiles, tomatoes, and herbs that cooks use to flavor just about everything: scrambled eggs, pinto beans, *arroz con pollo* (chicken and rice), and *mofongo* (mashed plantains).

Even simple foods are tropical treats. In the capital city of San Juan, Puerto Ricans enjoy pomelo, which looks like a gigantic grapefruit. Barceloneta grows so much pineapple that it's known as *La Ciudad de las Piñas*: Pineapple City. In Luquillo, kiosks sell stuffed savory pastries, fish and lobster, fried plantains, and refreshing fruit drinks right on the beach.

RICO

LEMONS, GRAPES, OLIVES

Spanish people brought citrus fruits, grapes, olives, and other Mediterranean flavors to Puerto Rico. Many of the island's stew and rice recipes have a strong Spanish influence.

CASSAVA ROOT

The cassava root is a little like a potato: inedible when raw, bland and starchy when cooked, and used in endless recipes! Puerto Ricans add it to stews, serve it fried or mashed with garlic, and even bake it into cookies at Christmas.

MOFONGO

Mofongo is made from green plantains that are fried, mashed, and shaped into a ball. Since Puerto Rico became an American territory, island cooks make a *mofongo* version of Thanksgiving stuffing, with turkey.

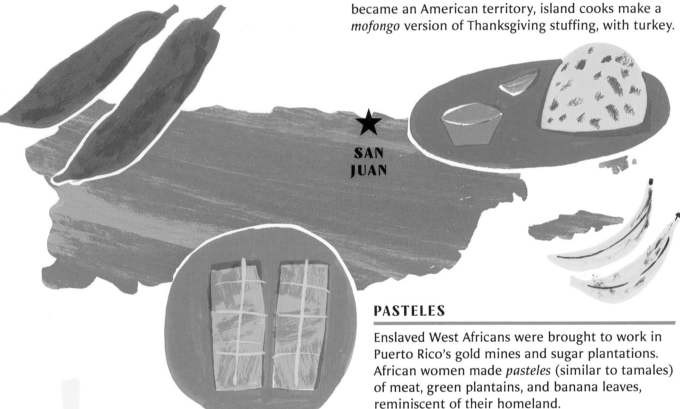

SAN JUAN

PASTELES

Enslaved West Africans were brought to work in Puerto Rico's gold mines and sugar plantations. African women made *pasteles* (similar to tamales) of meat, green plantains, and banana leaves, reminiscent of their homeland.

PERNIL

Pork is popular in Puerto Rico. In a dish called *pernil*, a pork shoulder is marinated and then slow cooked until it's meltingly tender. *Chicharrones* are pieces of pork skin fried until crisp.

Salt Cod Salad (Ensalada de Bacalao)

PREPARATION TIME	COOKING TIME	LEVEL OF DIFFICULTY	SERVES
35 minutes, plus 8 hours soaking time	20 minutes	● ● ○	4

Bacalao is the Spanish word for salt cod. Fresh fish spoils fast, so people developed this method of preserving it in lots of salt hundreds of years ago. You can find salt cod (often in wooden boxes) in the seafood section of large groceries and supermarkets.

INGREDIENTS

1 pound bacalao (salt cod)
3 medium potatoes, peeled and cubed
2 chayotes, cubed
1 large red onion, finely chopped
2 medium tomatoes, finely chopped
½ cup olive oil
3 tablespoons vinegar
1 teaspoon dried Mexican oregano
Coarse salt and freshly ground black pepper
Cooked white rice, for serving
2 ripe but firm avocados, peeled, pitted, and sliced
4 hard-boiled large eggs, peeled and sliced

1. Rinse the salt cod under cold running water, place in a large bowl, and cover with cold water. Soak for 8 hours. Rinse the cod again under cold running water for several minutes, and then transfer to a large pot. Cover the fish with water, bring to a boil, and drain. Repeat this boiling and draining process two more times.

2. In the same pot, place the drained cod and plenty of water to cover. Bring to a boil, and then add the potatoes and chayotes. Return to a boil and cook until the vegetables are tender, about 10 minutes. Drain everything in a colander.

3. Separate the cod from the vegetables. Transfer the vegetables to a large bowl and add the onion, tomatoes, oil, vinegar, and oregano. With a fork, flake the fish, removing any bones, and add to the bowl. Mix well and season to taste with salt and pepper.

4. Arrange the salad on top of cooked rice. Top with slices of avocado and hard-boiled eggs, and serve.

Eating in RHODE

When people from Portugal moved to America, many found a home in a little state that, like their mother country, looks out across the ocean: Rhode Island. Nationwide, America has only a tiny Portuguese population. But in Rhode Island, nearly ten percent of residents are Portuguese-Americans.

With more than 400 miles of coastline, Rhode Island is nicknamed the Ocean State. Immigrants from Portugal (which itself has over a thousand miles of Atlantic coast) have been moving to Rhode Island for hundreds of years. In that time, they brought their favorite recipes, many featuring fresh seafood. Look for grilled octopus, clam cakes, seafood-topped pasta, and a Mediterranean-influenced specialty called snail salad, made from the giant, spiral-shelled "sea snail" (also called conch), which is boiled, chopped, and mixed with olives, onions, garlic, and celery.

But Portuguese recipes in Rhode Island don't all contain seafood. There's also kale soup with spicy linguica sausage (known as *caldo verde*), *bitoque* (a little sirloin steak) and *feijoada* (black beans stewed with pork feet, knuckles, and sausage), as well as sweet-salty pastries such as *pasteis de nata* (custard tarts). Thanks to all these Portuguese treats, the littlest state is home to some very big flavors. As they say in Portuguese, it's *delicioso*!

ISLAND

"SOUPY" SAUSAGE

The town of Westerly is famous for something simply called "soupy": a peppery pork sausage first made by immigrants from Calabria, Italy.

JOHNNYCAKES

Johnnycakes are an old-fashioned Rhode Island breakfast made of white cornmeal. They are like a cross between small pancakes and English muffins.

CALDO VERDE

Portuguese immigrants make a hearty soup called *caldo verde*. A mix of kale, beans, and spicy sausage, it's the perfect warmer in a winter storm, like a nor'easter.

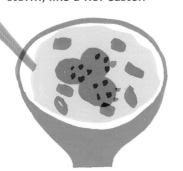

QUAHOGS

The official shellfish is the quahog (pronounced "KO-hog"), a clam that's excellent in chowder. Rhode Islanders invented a dish called clams casino, stuffed with bacon and breadcrumbs and served on the half shell.

PROVIDENCE

RHODE ISLAND CHOWDER

Taste the Ocean State in clear clam chowder: a steaming, sea-salty broth with potatoes and quahogs or cherrystone clams—hold the cream!

RHODE ISLAND RED

The state bird is a breed of chicken called the Rhode Island Red. They lay excellent eggs.

Coffee Cabinet

PREPARATION TIME	COOKING TIME	LEVEL OF DIFFICULTY	SERVES
15 minutes	20 minutes	● ○ ○	2

If somebody in Rhode Island offers you a coffee cabinet, don't worry—it's not a piece of furniture. The state's coffee-loving Italian-Americans use coffee-flavored syrup in drinks and desserts of all kinds. Add it to ice cream and milk—blended in a mixer kept in the cabinet—and you have the perfect summertime treat. The milkshake with the strange name is a favorite of kids and grown-ups alike!

INGREDIENTS
1 cup strong coffee
    (decaffeinated, if desired)
¾ cup sugar
1 pint coffee ice cream
¼ cup milk, or more to taste

SPECIAL EQUIPMENT
blender

1. To make syrup, in a small heavy-bottomed saucepan, bring the coffee and sugar just to a boil, stirring constantly. Reduce to a simmer and cook, stirring occasionally, for 15 minutes. Let cool.

2. Blend 2 tablespoons of the syrup with the ice cream and milk in a blender until smooth. Pour into 2 chilled glasses and serve. (Leftover syrup can be stored in the refrigerator for up to 1 month.)

Eating in SOUTH CAROLINA

South Carolina's coast is a lush wetland of swamps, creeks, winding rivers, grassy savannas, and saltwater marshes. Travel a hundred miles inland and you'll hit hills, pines, and pork, but the coastal Low Country is a place all its own, with its own foods, known as Low Country cuisine.

Low Country recipes use ingredients that thrive in these salty swamps. That means crab, shrimp, oysters, and fish, like porgy and bass, for breakfast, lunch, and dinner. The Low Country is a difficult place to grow crops like wheat, but it's perfect for rice, the star of many meals. Long-grain rice is served as a side, cooked with tomatoes into pilau, or simmered with chicken and sausage for a dish called chicken bog.

Many enslaved Africans were brought to the Low Country, and you can still taste their influences today. Visit historic Charleston, the beautiful city in the heart of the Low Country, and you'll find traditional dishes including okra soup and the black-eyed pea recipe called Hoppin' John at well-known restaurants.

But you don't need to be an award-winning chef to cook this cuisine. Just simmer up a Low Country boil, invite friends, and savor fresh seafood overlooking the marsh where it lived.

OKRA SOUP

The Gullah Geechee people live in the Sea Islands of South Carolina. Many of their traditions come from West Africa, including foods such as red rice and okra soup.

COLLARD GREENS

The state vegetable of South Carolina is collard greens. Slow-simmered until soft, they're often seasoned with pork, sugar, and vinegar.

BENNE WAFERS

Benne wafers are special South Carolina cookies filled with sesame seeds.

COLUMBIA ★

BOILED PEANUTS

Soft, salty boiled peanuts are South Carolina's official state snack.

SHRIMP BURGER

People here love shrimp so much, they even make shrimp burgers!

CHITTERLINGS AND HOT SAUCE

Chitterlings (pronounced "CHIT-lins") are a soul food staple. The boiled pig intestines are served with vinegar and hot sauce.

FROGMORE STEW

This stew contains no frogs! Instead, the big boil of the Carolina coast includes sweet corn, sausage, red potatoes, and shrimp.

Buttermilk Pie

PREPARATION TIME	COOKING TIME	LEVEL OF DIFFICULTY	SERVES
55 minutes (includes 30 minutes dough chilling time)	50 minutes	● ○ ○	8

Have you heard the phrase "easy as pie"? Well this pie is about the easiest example there is. Simply stir together a few ingredients, pour into a crust, and pop it in the oven. This delicious sweet and tart pie is enjoyed in South Carolina and all over the South.

INGREDIENTS

For dough:

1¼ cups all-purpose flour, plus more for work surface and your hands
1 teaspoon sugar
½ teaspoon salt
1 stick cold unsalted butter, cut into ½-inch cubes
3–4 tablespoons ice water

For filling:

1 cup sugar
3 tablespoons all-purpose flour
3 large eggs
1 cup buttermilk
1 stick unsalted butter, melted
2 teaspoons finely grated lemon zest
2 tablespoons fresh lemon juice
1 teaspoon pure vanilla extract

SPECIAL EQUIPMENT

rolling pin, 8- or 9-inch pie plate

1. Make the dough: In a large bowl, whisk together the flour, sugar, and salt. With a pastry blender or your fingertips, quickly work the butter into the dry ingredients until the mixture resembles coarse cornmeal. (You want the butter to be blended in but not completely: the small pieces are what make the crust flaky.) Add just enough ice water to bring the dough together—begin by adding 3 tablespoons, blend in, and then add more only if necessary. You can test it by taking a handful of dough and squeezing it: The dough should be neither wet, nor dry and crumbly.

2. Using your hands, form the dough into a ball. Flatten it into a disk, wrap with plastic wrap, and refrigerate until firm, at least 30 minutes.

3. Lightly flour a work surface and place the chilled dough on it. Using floured hands, flatten dough slightly. Dust the rolling pin with flour, and roll from the center outward using light, even pressure. Roll until the dough is about ¼-inch thick and 10–11 inches in diameter. Drape the pastry over the rolling pin and place it in the pie plate. Press firmly into the bottom and sides of the pan. Use a paring knife to trim the dough, leaving at least ½ inch of overhang all around. Crimp the edges using the side of your forefinger and thumb, or the tines of a fork to press down along the edge. Freeze the pie shell for 10 minutes (or refrigerate for 30 minutes).

4. Position a rack in the middle of the oven and preheat to 350°F.

5. Make the filling: In a medium bowl, whisk together the sugar and flour. Whisk in the eggs. Blend in the buttermilk, melted butter, lemon zest, lemon juice, and vanilla until smooth.

6. Pour the filling into the pie shell. Bake until the filling is just set, 40–45 minutes. Transfer to a wire rack and let the pie cool to room temperature before serving.

Eating in SOUTH DAKOTA

Have you *herd*? The Mount Rushmore State is perfect for raising herds of livestock. After all, the Great Plains were the bison's native habitat. Talk about free range!

Today, farmers have put up fences and the plains are home to big cattle ranches. A favorite dinner is the Hot Beef Combo — that's mashed potatoes, roast beef, and white bread, all bathed in homemade gravy. It will warm you up in even the coldest South Dakota blizzard.

Food here isn't all bison and beef. Some ranchers raise sheep. Hunters cook wild pheasant. And South Dakotans love to snack on something called Tiger Meat, but don't worry, it's not the giant striped cat. Instead the "tiger" is raw beef, raw egg, and raw onion, mixed with salt and pepper and served on crackers.

Corn and soybeans are important crops to feed to all those herds, so livestock farmers rely on the state's grain growers. Every year South Dakotans celebrate these farms at the World's Only Corn Palace in Mitchell, where artists use 13 different colors of corn to make huge murals covering the outside of the arena! Now that's some tasteful art!

COFFEE 5¢
WALL DRUG

WALL DRUG BILLBOARD

For generations, interstate drivers have stopped at Wall Drug, the landmark store and eatery, for a snack or a meal.

BISON

Native people of the Great Plains relied on bison herds as their main food. Today, the meat is cooked into delicious burgers in towns named Bison and Buffalo.

PIERRE
★

PEMMICAN

The Lakota and other Native people ate pemmican, made from chokecherries and bison meat. Think of it as the original energy bar.

CHISLIC

South Dakotans eat kebabs called *chislic*, bites of red meat (beef, lamb, or venison) that are skewered and fried.

KUCHEN

German immigrants brought kuchen to the prairie. The yeasted cake can be flavored with fruits or sweet custard, and is the official state dessert.

Norwegian Meatballs

PREPARATION TIME	COOKING TIME	LEVEL OF DIFFICULTY	SERVES
15 minutes	35 minutes	● ● ○	4–6

In the 1800s, many Norwegian farmers moved to the Dakotas and by 1889, a third of South Dakota's population were people from Norway. They brought recipes like these meatballs, cooked in a creamy sauce and seasoned with warming spices (nutmeg and ginger). They're often served over mashed root vegetables, like potatoes or rutabagas, with jellied cranberries on the side. Try them for yourself, and imagine that you're in South Dakota, hunkering down for a blizzard.

INGREDIENTS

2 pounds ground beef
2 large eggs
¾ cup fresh breadcrumbs
¾ cup milk
2 tablespoons minced onion
1 teaspoon freshly ground black pepper
1 teaspoon salt
½ teaspoon ground ginger
¼ teaspoon freshly grated nutmeg
4 tablespoons butter
2 tablespoons all-purpose flour
2 cups beef stock, preferably low-sodium

1. In a large bowl, mix the beef, eggs, breadcrumbs, milk, onion, pepper, salt, ginger, and nutmeg. Blend thoroughly, using your hands at first, then a spoon for several minutes. (You can also use an electric mixer for this: it makes a lighter meatball.) Using your hands, form the meat mixture into 12 balls the size of golf balls.

2. In a large frying pan, melt 2 tablespoons of the butter over medium-high heat. Add 6 of the meatballs and cook, turning so they brown evenly, about 5 minutes. (They should still be pink inside, because they will cook further in the next step.) Transfer to a plate. Repeat with the remaining 2 tablespoons butter and 6 meatballs, transferring the browned meatballs to the plate.

3. Reduce the heat to medium and stir the flour into the pan. Add the beef stock, whisking until smooth. Add the meatballs to the sauce, and reduce the heat to medium-low. Cover, and simmer until cooked through, about 25 minutes. Serve immediately.

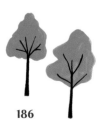

Eating in

TENNE

Memphis is called the "Home of the Blues" and Nashville is known as "Music City, USA." But even if you don't have rhythm, be sure you can count to three. Because "meat-and-three" restaurants are some of the best places to eat in Tennessee.

At meat-and-threes, you grab a tray and choose a meat and three side dishes. It sounds simple, but it's difficult with so many choices! For "meat," you'll see pork chops, fried chicken, cured ham, and fried shrimp. But the "three" is where things get really interesting: turnip greens, creamed corn, buttery cabbage, fried okra, corn pudding, crowder peas, mac and cheese, and even Jell-O. If those don't fill you up, choose a sweet, too—like banana pudding, sweet potato pie, or caramel cake.

Sometimes you'll find barbecue at a meat-and-three restaurant. After all, experts call Memphis one of the best barbecue cities in America. And the annual Memphis in May festival is one of the biggest barbecue contests anywhere. Pit masters come from across the country, but many live right in Memphis, where they've perfected slow-smoked pork. The most popular thing to order is ribs, rubbed with tongue-tingling spices, or barbecued-pork sandwiches. People here are so crazy for barbecued pork that they pile it on salads, spaghetti, nachos—even pizza!

BBQ SANDWICH

The classic Memphis sandwich features barbecued pork and a tangy red sauce, piled on a bun and topped with coleslaw.

WILD LEEKS

"Tennessee truffles" are wild leeks (also called ramps) that grow all over the Appalachian Mountains.

HOT CHICKEN

Hot chicken is a super-spicy fried chicken that's unique to Nashville.

NASHVILLE

SPAGHETTI WITH BARBECUE SAUCE

People in Memphis put barbecue sauce on spaghetti!

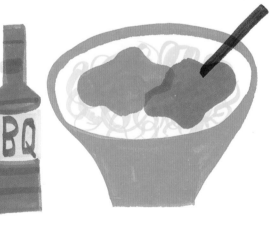

REDEYE GRAVY

This sauce, made from country ham drippings and a bit of coffee, is poured over ham and biscuits for breakfast.

COUNTRY HAM

Tennessee country hams are famous for their deep, smoky flavor. They sometimes "cure," or air-dry, for up to two years before they are ready to eat.

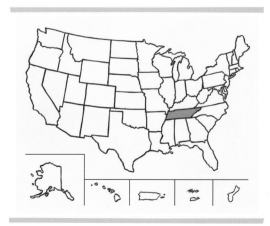

189

Buttermilk Cornbread

PREPARATION TIME	COOKING TIME	LEVEL OF DIFFICULTY	SERVES
10 minutes	20 minutes	● ○ ○	4–6

Up in New England, people like their cornbread sweet. Out in the Southwest, they add spicy green chiles. Throughout the South, cornbread recipes feature buttermilk. Some have corn kernels, bacon, or pork cracklings added to the batter, but never sugar or spice. Almost all southern cornbread has one thing in common, however: it's baked in a cast-iron skillet, most likely one made in the state of Tennessee.

INGREDIENTS
2 tablespoons canola oil
1½ cups medium or stone-
    ground cornmeal
1 cup all-purpose flour
2 teaspoons baking powder
¾ teaspoon coarse salt
2 large eggs
1 cup buttermilk
4 tablespoons unsalted
    butter, melted

SPECIAL EQUIPMENT
a 9-inch cast-iron skillet

1. Preheat the oven to 425°F. Brush the oil over the bottom and sides of the skillet and place in the oven to heat.

2. Meanwhile, in a large bowl, whisk together the cornmeal, flour, baking powder, sugar, and salt. Make a well in the center of the ingredients, add the eggs, and lightly beat them in. Add the buttermilk and melted butter and stir just until the dry ingredients are evenly moistened.

3. Carefully remove the hot skillet from the oven and quickly pour the batter into it. Put it back into the oven and bake just until the sides pull away from the pan and the center of the bread springs back when pressed, about 20 minutes. Transfer the skillet to a wire rack and let cool. Serve cornbread warm or at room temperature, right from the skillet.

Eating in TEXAS

Nothing says "Texas" like the official state dish: a bowl of chili. While people in other parts of the country add everything from turkey to zucchini, there's no messing with chili here: it's beef and chile peppers. You could say these two ingredients are the culinary stars of the Lone Star State. According to Lyndon B. Johnson, a Texan who became the 36th US President, "chili concocted outside of Texas is a weak, apologetic imitation of the real thing."

Texas is the country's top beef producer, with ranches in each of this huge state's 254 counties. Barbecued brisket is one of the most popular ways of preparing beef here. Texans also enjoy beef in sizzling fajitas, enchiladas, and chicken-fried steak.

The border with Mexico lends its name to a type of food that's popular all over the US: Tex-Mex. Cooks along the border have always seasoned foods with dried ground chile peppers. Today, they still use chiles to flavor meals from breakfast (scrambled eggs and crumbled tortillas, called *migas*) to dessert (spicy chocolate cakes and cookies).

BEEF

Texas ranchers raise more than 10 million cattle each year. Some of the meat becomes slow-cooked barbecued brisket, first popularized by German and Czech immigrants.

CHILE CON QUESO

Chile con queso is a bowl of melted cheese flavored with chiles. It's served with salty tortilla chips, for dipping.

RED GRAPEFRUIT

Farmers have grown grapefruit in Texas since the 1700s. In 1929, one tree evolved to bear sweet, red grapefruit, now the official state fruit.

AUSTIN

FRITO PIE

Texans pour chili and cheese right into a small, split-open bag of Fritos at Friday night football. That's Frito pie—better use napkins!

JUNETEENTH

For more than 150 years, Texans have celebrated the end of slavery on June 19th. Juneteenth picnics feature black-eyed peas, pulled pork, strawberry soda, and a "new dawn" flag.

BARBACOA

In Southern Texas, cow heads are buried with hot coals in the ground to make a kind of barbecue called *barbacoa*.

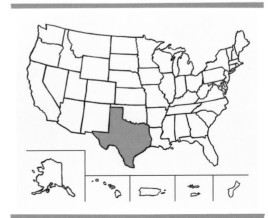

Potato, Egg, and Bacon Breakfast Tacos

PREPARATION TIME	COOKING TIME	LEVEL OF DIFFICULTY	SERVES
10 minutes	25 minutes	● ● ○	2

Texans love tacos so much, they eat them for breakfast! People in Mexico have long topped tortillas with eggs; this recipe (especially popular in Central Texas and in Austin, the state capital) honors that tradition and adds a few American morning favorites: potatoes, cheese, and bacon. A shake of hot sauce or a dollop of salsa will carry your taste buds straight to the Lone Star State.

INGREDIENTS
4 slices thick-cut bacon
1 russet (baking) potato or 8 fingerlings (about 8 ounces), cut into ½-inch slices
Coarse salt and freshly ground black pepper
Large pinch of paprika (optional)
2 large eggs, lightly beaten
4 corn or flour tortillas (6-inch), warmed according to package directions
Optional toppings: salsa, finely chopped onion, cubed avocado, hot sauce, fresh cilantro

1. Heat a large cast-iron skillet over medium-high until hot. Add the bacon and cook, turning occasionally, until the fat is frothy and the bacon is crisp, 4–6 minutes. Place the bacon on a paper towel-covered plate. (Keep the skillet with about 2 tablespoons of the bacon fat in it.) When cool enough to handle, crumble the bacon.

2. Return the skillet to heat, add the potato, and season with salt, pepper, and paprika, if using. Cook, partially covered, until golden brown and tender, 10–12 minutes. Using a slotted spoon, transfer the potatoes to a bowl.

3. Return the pan to medium heat, add the eggs, and season with salt and pepper. Scramble the eggs, pushing them around with a spoon, until they are fluffy and cooked to your liking, 1–2 minutes.

4. To serve, top each flat tortilla with crumbled bacon, scrambled eggs, and potatoes. Serve with desired toppings.

Eating in the U.S. VIRGIN

When you live on the Caribbean islands, you're literally surrounded by seafood. People eat saltfish for breakfast, and "pot fish" (so called because they were once caught in pots) for dinner. But fish aren't the only seafood: locals love the sea snail called conch, which divers collect from the ocean floor. Cooks sauté the meat in butter or fry it into fritters, and serve it with a dipping sauce of ketchup, mayonnaise, lime juice, and hot sauce. Islanders enjoy soft-tail Caribbean crabs, too.

You can taste the Islands' history in its recipes. Many enslaved people, brought here to harvest sugarcane, introduced African flavors. Okra and greens are still popular in *kallaloo*, a dish served throughout the Caribbean, and served here with *fungi* (pronounced FOON-ji), a thick cornmeal mash with okra that's as common here as mashed potatoes are in the Midwest. Immigrants from India brought curries, flatbreads called rotis, and deep-fried savory pastries called *pate* to the islands. Today, curried goat is a common dinner, often doused with sauce made from super-spicy Scotch bonnet peppers.

When you're ready to cool off, grab a refreshing fizzy mauby soda made from tree bark, cold sea-moss tea, or puckery passion fruit juice.

ISLANDS

CHARLOTTE AMALIE ★

DUMB BREAD

In the US Virgin Islands, it's smart to eat "dumb bread." Introduced by servants from India, the shortcake-style breads are cooked in a skillet over hot coals.

RØDGRØD

Before they became a US territory in 1916, these islands were home to Danish sugar plantations. While here, Danes made their traditional fruit sauce, called *rødgrød*, with tropical ingredients such as guava and tapioca.

"FUNGI"

Fungi here isn't a mushroom—it's boiled cornmeal cooked with okra. The dish was favored by Africans brought as slaves, and is still served with fish today.

JERK CHICKEN

Jerk cooking is a kind of barbecue you find all around the Caribbean. Meats, especially chicken, are covered in a sweet, hot mix of spices.

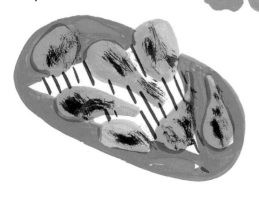

GOAT WATER

Goat water isn't a drink for livestock. It's a hearty stew made of goat meat, fruit (pawpaw and breadfruit), and fiery peppers known as Scotch bonnets.

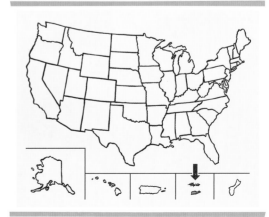

Yellow Rice and Pigeon Peas

PREPARATION TIME	COOKING TIME	LEVEL OF DIFFICULTY	SERVES
15 minutes	1 hour	● ● ○	8

Pigeon peas are tiny beans popular in Africa and India. The flavors of this rice dish are a mix of Spanish, African, and native Caribbean cuisines, which reflect the island's diversity and history. It takes on a beautiful golden color from the annatto, which you can find in most Latin groceries. If you can't find it, you can leave it out or substitute ¼ teaspoon ground turmeric. The tomato paste will also color the rice.

INGREDIENTS

1 small green bell pepper, seeded and coarsely chopped
1 small red bell pepper, seeded and coarsely chopped
½ medium onion, coarsely chopped
2 garlic cloves, coarsely chopped
½ cup coarsely chopped cilantro
¼ cup vegetable oil
1 (4-ounce) piece smoked ham, diced
2 tablespoons tomato paste
1 teaspoon ground annatto (or ¼ teaspoon ground turmeric)
½ cup sliced pimiento-stuffed olives
1 tablespoon capers, drained and rinsed
2 cups long-grain white rice
1 can (15 ounces) pigeon peas, drained and rinsed
Coarse salt

SPECIAL EQUIPMENT
a food processor

1. Place the green pepper, red pepper, onion, garlic, and cilantro in a food processor and pulse to a paste (this is called a *sofrito*).

2. Cut out a round of wax paper slightly larger than the diameter of a wide, heavy pot with a tight-fitting lid. In the same pot, heat the oil over medium-high. Add the ham and cook, stirring occasionally, until it starts to crisp, about 4 minutes. Add the *sofrito*, tomato paste, annatto (or turmeric), olives, and capers and cook, stirring, until liquid has evaporated, about 3 minutes. Add the rice and cook, stirring, until it sizzles, about 2 minutes.

3. Stir in the peas, 3½ cups water, and 1 teaspoon salt and bring to a simmer. Simmer, uncovered, over medium-high heat until almost all of liquid is absorbed, about 10 minutes, reducing the heat to medium when the water is below the level of the rice.

4. Gently stir the rice mixture from bottom to top, then smooth the top so it's even. Place the wax paper round directly on top of rice mixture and cover pot with the lid. Reduce heat to low and cook without stirring, 30 minutes.

5. Remove the pot from the heat, carefully remove the lid, and discard the paper. Gently fluff rice with a fork. Cover the pot with lid and let stand 10 minutes. Season with more salt, if desired, and serve.

Eating in UTAH

Mormon pioneers crossed the American West in 1847, herding cattle and pulling handcarts on the 1,300-mile walk to Utah. But upon arriving, they had little more to eat than what remained of the porridge, hominy, and molasses they'd bought at the last trading post. Native Americans showed them the sego lily, a wild plant whose edible roots they dug and roasted to keep from starving.

These days, hungry Utah residents can run to the supermarket rather than dig up lily roots. But food storage and preparedness are still very important to the Mormon community. Recalling their ancestors' near-starvation, many are inspired to keep a year's supply of food in storage for their families. Community gatherings feature generous servings of creamy casseroles (especially potato), salads (seven-layer is a favorite, as is anything made with Jell-O), and other hearty fare to make sure everyone leaves full. Church suppers and family gatherings feature foods that can feed a crowd, from frog-eye salad (made with the tiny pasta shapes called *acini de pepe)* to ambrosia, a dessert salad filled with mini marshmallows, mandarin orange slices, and shredded coconut. In summer, locals feast on sweet Green River melons and snack on squares of sticky fudge.

BEEHIVE

The hardworking honeybee is the official state insect of the Beehive State. Beehives appear on Utah's state flag and state seal.

PINK SALT

The town of Redmond is home to a salt deposit left over from when the ocean covered the area more than two million years ago. The salt is pink and delicious.

TUMBLEWEED GREENS

A remote restaurant in the tiny town of Boulder (population 226) serves desert ingredients such as baby tumbleweed greens.

★
SALT LAKE CITY

FRY SAUCE

Move over, plain ketchup. Here in Utah, people serve their French fries with fry sauce, a mixture of ketchup and mayo.

FUNERAL POTATOES

This cheesy, buttery, baked casserole, made with hash browns and topped with potato chips or cornflakes, is served at funerals (and nearly every other community gathering).

RASPBERRY SHAKE

Every summer, Bear Lake raspberries are ripe for the picking. Locals blend them into the area's famous shakes.

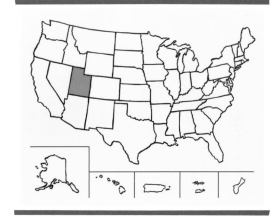

Green Jell-O Salad

PREPARATION TIME	COOKING TIME	LEVEL OF DIFFICULTY	SERVES
10 minutes, plus 30 minutes chilling and 2–3 hours setting time	5 minutes	● ○ ○	12

Jell-O plays a big role in Utah cooking. It can be layered or molded, served as a salad, a dessert, or even a main dish, depending on what's suspended within it or floating on top. Utahans stir in all kinds of ingredients, like shredded carrots, kidney beans, pretzels, canned mandarin orange segments, and mini marshmallows, just to name a few favorites. You'll see this traditional jiggly salad at buffets and community gatherings all over the state.

INGREDIENTS
1 box (3 ounces) lime Jell-O
1 box (3 ounces) lemon Jell-O
1 can (8 ounces) juice-packed crushed pineapple
1 cup full-fat cottage cheese
½ cup mayonnaise

1. Empty the boxes of Jell-O powders into a large heatproof bowl.

2. Drain the pineapple liquid into a 2-cup measuring cup and set the fruit aside. Add enough water to the juice to measure 2 cups, pour into a saucepan, and bring to a boil. Pour into the bowl of Jell-O powders and stir to dissolve.

3. Transfer bowl to the refrigerator. Chill until the mixture has thickened to the consistency of thick syrup, about 30 minutes.

4. Stir in the pineapple, cottage cheese, and mayonnaise until completely incorporated. Pour the mixture into a medium-sized mold or bowl, or a few small bowls. Cover and refrigerate until set, 2–3 hours. Turn out of mold by flipping it upside down onto a plate larger than the mold, and serve.

Eating in VERMO

People in Vermont have many reasons to celebrate the end of winter. But the biggest reason is maple syrup. Sure, people make maple syrup from Maine to Michigan—but Vermont makes the most, and many say they make the *best*.

Maple syrup can only be made from sugar maple trees, which grow across the Green Mountains that give the state its name (from the French: *vert* for green and *mont* for mountains.) Sugar maples store sugar in their roots and, when they feel winter's thaw, they send sap up to feed spring's buds. If you've tapped a hole into the trunk, some of it will run out and into your waiting bucket.

So, each March, Vermonters trudge through the snow to tap trees. As buckets fill with sap, people bring them into little buildings called "sugar shacks," where they boil the sap down into thick, sweet maple syrup. For the next month, sugar maple "tappers" collect and boil sap around the clock. Puffs of smoke rise from the Green Mountains, as everyone races the warming weather. In a few weeks, the buds will swell, the sap will change, the holes will heal, and the buckets will be put away. But there will be enough syrup to drizzle over pancakes, flavor baked beans, and fill maple cream pies all year long.

MAPLE SYRUP

To make one gallon of maple syrup takes about 40 gallons of raw sap.

TOURTIÈRE

Tourtière is a meat-and-potato pie brought to Vermont by French Canadians. Cooks use rabbit, pork, beef, or even wild game meat in the filling, depending on what they can get.

★

MONTPELIER

DAIRY COW

Each year, Vermont's dairy cows produce enough milk to fill 16,000 swimming pools!

MAPLE CANDY

Vermont's "sugar bush" produces more than maple syrup. Maple candy, maple cream, and taffy called "sugar on snow" are favorites in the Green Mountain State.

FIDDLEHEAD FERNS

One of the first foods of spring is the wild fiddlehead fern, picked when it's a curled-up coil smaller than your fist. People cook them in butter to toss with pasta or eat over toast.

APPLE PIE WITH CHEESE

Vermont creameries make some of the best cheddar cheese in the nation. Vermonters enjoy it on slices of apple pie!

Maple-Glazed Brussels Sprouts with Bacon

PREPARATION TIME	COOKING TIME	LEVEL OF DIFFICULTY	SERVES
15 minutes	30 mknutes	● ○ ○	8

Dinner may be a little sweeter in Vermont, where local maple syrup is still on the table long past breakfast. This salty-sweet side dish features Brussels sprouts, which look like tiny little cabbages and are especially tasty when paired with bacon. Serve it alongside the turkey for a taste of a Yankee-style Thanksgiving, or try it any night of the year.

INGREDIENTS

1 pound bacon, cut into
    1-inch pieces
2 pounds Brussels sprouts,
    halved lengthwise
¼ cup pure maple syrup
Salt and freshly ground
    black pepper

1. In a large skillet, cook the bacon over medium-high heat until crisp, about 10 minutes. Remove the bacon with a slotted spoon, leaving the bacon fat in the pan.

2. Add the sprouts and cook over medium heat, stirring, until golden brown and barely tender, about 15 minutes. Add the maple syrup and cook for another 5 minutes, stirring occasionally.

3. Toss in the bacon and season to taste with salt and pepper. Serve immediately.

Eating in VIRGI

Virginia has two nicknames. It's called the "Old Dominion," because the colony was a dominion, or territory, of the English king and queen. It's also known as the "Mother of Presidents," because four of America's first five presidents came from Virginia. Yet Virginia's foods were shaped most of all by people who were neither royalty nor presidents. They were slaves.

America's Founding Father farmers, including Washington, Jefferson, Madison, and Monroe, lived on large Virginia plantations with impressive gardens and kitchens. Their corn, wheat, and pork produced some of the finest dining in the young country. But these gentleman farmers didn't do it alone. Each enslaved many Africans who shouldered the work in the fields and at the stove.

Today, farms and restaurants are owned by black and white Virginians. But you can taste history on modern menus. Traditional recipes such as cured ham, Brunswick stew, fried chicken, collard greens, crab imperial, fried oysters, black-eyed peas, and peanut pie are all still beloved. They're often prepared by people whose skilled-but-enslaved ancestors cooked these foods for presidents. Today, though, they're made by choice. And they taste best when we all sit at the table together.

FRIED CHICKEN

After the Civil War, African-American women in Gordonsville sold homemade meals to passengers on passing trains. Today, the town's annual festival celebrates its history as "Chicken Leg Center of the Universe."

BRUNSWICK STEW

This smoky, thick, tomato-based dish is filled with beans, okra, chicken, and wild game (often rabbit or squirrel).

CORN OYSTERS

Golden-fried corn fritters, often called "corn oysters" for their shape and size, have been popular since colonial days. They are still a traditional side dish at Thanksgiving.

SALLY LUNN BREAD

At Colonial Williamsburg, you can experience 18th-century America, complete with time travel tastes like Sally Lunn bread, a sweet, rich, yeasted treat.

★
RICHMOND

VIRGINIA PEANUTS

Virginia (or "ballpark") peanuts are the biggest of all varieties. Try them southern-style: boiled and salted in the shell!

OYSTERS

All East Coast oysters are the same species: the delicious *Crassostrea virginica*, also known as the Virginia oyster. They vary in size and taste based on the water they grow in. Plump, briny Tidewater oysters have been served to many presidents.

AMERICA'S FIRST WAFFLES

At Monticello, Thomas Jefferson's restored home, you can tour his incredible gardens and visit the kitchen where he introduced Americans to waffles, macaroni and cheese, and ice cream.

COUNTRY HAM

In Colonial Virginia, country ham was cured with so much salt that it could go unrefrigerated for months. At Mount Vernon, Martha Washington cured 400 hams per year. Smithfield Hams in Hampton Roads still sells the smoky, salty pork.

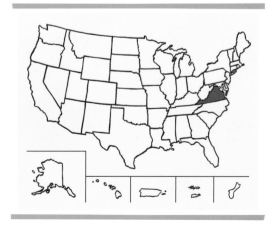

Peanut Soup

PREPARATION TIME	COOKING TIME	LEVEL OF DIFFICULTY	SERVES
10 minutes	35 minutes	● ● ○	6–8

Before there was peanut butter and jelly, there was peanut soup. The peanut is native to South America, but was carried around the world on the ships of Spanish and Portuguese explorers. In Virginia, enslaved people cooked the nuts into stews that eventually became popular in restaurants, too. Farmers here still grow lots of peanuts, and you can still order a bowl of peanut soup.

INGREDIENTS

4 tablespoons unsalted butter
1 medium onion, finely chopped
2 stalks celery, finely chopped
3 tablespoons all-purpose flour
6 cups chicken stock, preferably low-sodium
2 cups smooth peanut butter
1½ cups heavy (whipping) cream
¼ cup chopped salted roasted peanuts

SPECIAL EQUIPMENT

a fine-mesh sieve

1. In a large saucepan, melt the butter over medium heat. Add the onion and celery and cook, stirring often, until softened, 3–5 minutes.

2. Stir in the flour and cook until lightly golden, about 3 minutes.

3. Pour in the chicken stock, increase the heat to high, and bring to a boil, stirring well to combine. Reduce the heat to medium and cook, stirring frequently, until slightly reduced and thickened, about 15 minutes.

4. Set a sieve over a large bowl and pour soup through it, straining out the solids. Return the liquid to the saucepan. Whisk the peanut butter and the cream into the liquid. Warm over low heat, whisking frequently, until warmed through, about 5 minutes. Do not boil.

5. Serve warm, garnished with chopped peanuts.

Eating in WASHING

Washington has a rainy reputation. It's home to seven of the wettest places in America, including Aberdeen, which receives over six feet of rain each year! Grab your raincoat—and your fork—to discover foods that are literally wet and wild.

More than half of Washington is covered with towering forests that get so much rainfall, they are *rain forests*. All that rain keeps things very green, earning Washington its nickname: the Evergreen State. Those lush evergreen regions are the best spots to forage for wild mushrooms—like morels, chanterelles, puffballs, and "chicken of the woods"—as well as water-loving wild blueberries, blackberries, cloudberries, and chokecherries.

Washington residents also eat from the water itself: the mighty Pacific Ocean! They cheer the annual return of salmon and steelhead trout, which swim in from the ocean to lay eggs in fresh water. Many people grill fish on cedar planks, sometimes right on the shore. Locals also feast on Dungeness crab and slurp briny raw oysters.

Not all of Washington is wet, though: east of its vast mountain ranges, the weather is dry, perfect for growing many of the apples, pears, cherries, and raspberries you see in supermarkets across the country.

...GTON

PEARS

Washington farms grow more pears than in any other state. Pears are the only orchard fruit that doesn't ripen on the tree.

CHICKEN TERIYAKI

One of Seattle's best-known dishes was developed by a Japanese-American. The rice, chicken, crunchy salad greens, and salty-sweet sauce are a mix of Japanese and American tastes.

COFFEE

Seattle is the nation's most caffeinated city. There are more coffee shops per person than in any other place in the US.

OLYMPIA ★

PUBLIC MARKET CENTER

PIKE PLACE MARKET

Fishmongers at Seattle's Pike Place Market shout out each order and throw fresh fish through the air!

STRAWBERRIES

In the late 1800s, many Japanese immigrants came to the Washington coast to start strawberry farms, turning the region into a berry paradise!

APLETS AND COTLETS

Central Washington's orchards grow prize-winning fruits, especially apples and apricots. Some people cook the harvests into sticky candies called aplets and cotlets.

WILD SALMON

Wild salmon hatch in freshwater streams and rivers. They migrate to the Pacific Ocean, before swimming back upstream again.

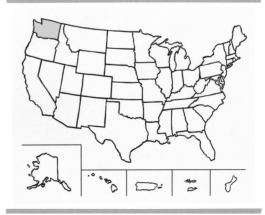

Dutch Baby Pancake

PREPARATION TIME	COOKING TIME	LEVEL OF DIFFICULTY	SERVES
5 minutes	15 minutes	● ○ ○	2

This skillet-baked breakfast was first popularized by a café in Seattle in the 1940s. Now it's a morning favorite throughout the state and the Pacific Northwest. The simple, rich pancake puffs up impressively in the oven—no flipping necessary. Top it with butter and syrup, lemon juice and powdered sugar, or fresh berries and whipped cream.

INGREDIENTS

4 tablespoons unsalted butter
3 large eggs
¼ cup milk
½ cup all-purpose flour
¼ cup sugar
Pinch of salt
Pinch of freshly grated nutmeg
½ teaspoon pure vanilla extract
½ lemon

1. Preheat the oven to 425°F. Place 3 tablespoons of the butter in a large ovenproof cast-iron skillet and place in the oven to preheat. Cut the remaining tablespoon of butter into small pieces, and set aside.

2. In a bowl, whisk together the eggs, milk, flour, 3 tablespoons sugar, the salt, nutmeg, and vanilla. Whisk vigorously for 1 minute, until the mixture is foamy.

3. Carefully remove the hot skillet from the oven and quickly pour the batter into it. Return to the oven, and bake until puffed up and lightly browned, 10–15 minutes.

4. Remove from the oven, quickly dot the pancake with the reserved butter pieces, and sprinkle with the remaining tablespoon sugar. Squeeze the lemon half over the top. Serve immediately.

Eating in WASHING[TON]

Our nation's capital draws people from across America and around the world. So the city, which borders Virginia, is seasoned with both Southern hospitality and international flair. Thanks to the immigrants who have settled here, people in the District can taste the flavors of the world without ever leaving town!

Important meetings with world leaders happen here all the time. Sometimes, special state dinners are held at the White House when the president welcomes a foreign dignitary. Usually, the White House chooses foods and entertainment to make the guests feel comfortable, like serving lamb for the president of Tunisia, homemade chutney for India's prime minister, and vegetables with lemongrass for Nelson Mandela!

Because Washington, DC, is home to so many embassies, you can find food from almost every country on earth. Today, even if you don't have an invitation to a White House state dinner, you can eat your way around the world. Find oniony stew from Yemen, cheesy *pupusas* from El Salvador, spicy beef salad from Laos, and Moroccan mint tea all within a few blocks.

INJERA BREAD

With America's largest concentration of immigrants from Ethiopia, Washington, DC, boasts many restaurants that serve spongy bread called injera, eaten with lentils, greens, yogurt, and spicy chicken or goat.

HALF-SMOKE

Washington locals enjoy a delicious sausage known as half-smoke. The combination of ground pork and beef in the same bun is a DC classic.

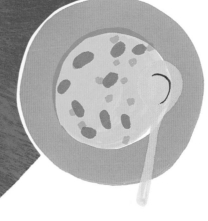

WHITE HOUSE CHINA

Presidents have been hosting foreign leaders since 1874, when Ulysses S. Grant welcomed King Kalakaua of the Sandwich Islands (now Hawaii). Dinners are served on formal White House china.

SENATE BEAN SOUP

This long-beloved recipe from the US Senate dining room is made with navy beans, ham hocks, and onions. Early versions included mashed potatoes!

MUMBO SAUCE

Mumbo sauce is made with tomatoes, vinegar, sugar, and sometimes nutmeg and sour cream. DC residents like to drizzle it over chicken wings, egg rolls, fried rice, and French fries.

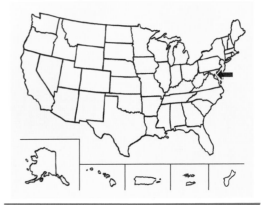

Chicken Bánh Mì

PREPARATION TIME	**COOKING TIME**	**LEVEL OF DIFFICULTY**	**MAKES**
30 minutes, plus 1 hour pickling and 30 minutes marinating	10 minutes	● ● ○	4 sandwiches

More than a million and a half people of Vietnamese descent live in America, but millions more have come to love this sandwich! The *bánh mì* takes southeast Asian flavors and ingredients, like pickled vegetables, mint, and cilantro, and stuffs them into baguettes (French bread), which were introduced in Vietnam when it was a French colony. *Bánh mì* sandwiches are often topped with roast pork, pâté, sardines, or tofu, so swap out the chicken for any other protein you prefer.

INGREDIENTS

For the pickles:
1 cup shredded carrots or carrot matchsticks
¼ cup plus 1 teaspoon sugar
½ teaspoon coarse salt
1 cup rice vinegar

For the chicken:
1 tablespoon Asian fish sauce
1 tablespoon fresh lime juice
1 tablespoon canola oil
½ teaspoon sugar
1 large garlic clove, smashed and peeled
¼ teaspoon coarse salt
1 pound boneless, skinless chicken thighs

For the sandwiches:
4 bánh mì rolls, mini hoagie rolls, or mini baguettes, halved lengthwise
Mayonnaise
4 cilantro sprigs, any thick stems removed
8 mint leaves, torn if large
1 small cucumber, cut lengthwise into 8 wedges
Sliced jalapeño (optional)

1. Make the pickles: In a bowl, toss the carrots with 1 teaspoon sugar and the salt. Let stand for 10 minutes, and then drain off excess liquid. Rinse the carrots and pat dry with paper towels.

2. Transfer the carrots to a quart-sized jar or plastic container. In a liquid measuring cup, combine remaining ¼ cup sugar with the vinegar and 1 cup water and whisk until the sugar dissolves. Pour this brine over the vegetables and let stand for at least 1 hour. (Pickled vegetables can be refrigerated, covered, for up to 2 weeks.)

3. Make the chicken: In a large bowl, stir to combine the fish sauce, lime juice, oil, sugar, garlic clove, and salt until the salt and sugar dissolve. Add the chicken and use tongs to turn and coat with the marinade. Let stand 30 minutes, or cover and refrigerate up to 4 hours.

4. Set a rack about 4 inches from the broiler and preheat the broiler to high. Cover a baking sheet with foil and arrange the chicken thighs on it in a single layer (discard marinade). Broil chicken until it starts to brown, about 5 minutes. Flip and broil until cooked through, about 5 minutes longer. Transfer chicken to a cutting board and let rest for 3 minutes. Cut chicken into thick slices.

5. Make the sandwiches: Spread the cut sides of the rolls with mayonnaise. Arrange chicken slices on bottom halves of rolls, then top with the mint and cilantro, pickled vegetables, cucumbers, and jalapeño, if using. Sandwich with top halves of rolls, and serve.

Eating in WEST VIR...

West Virginia is known as the Mountain State, and here in the beautiful Appalachian Mountains, you'll find limestone caves, cool streams, thick forests, and fertile river bottoms. By expertly foraging, hunting, preserving, and persevering, families in Appalachia have feasted on the mountains' bounty for centuries.

West Virginians celebrate spring with ramps, wild leeks that pop up from the forest floor. In summer, families pick morel mushrooms, creasy greens (a type of watercress), leaf lettuce (delicious cooked in bacon fat), and wild blackberries. Many families still follow Grandma's recipe for squirrel stew, or work magic with pickling, canning, and other ways to "put food by," preserving it to last for months. Desserts are sweetened with sorghum, a tall plant that gets simmered into sticky syrup each fall.

West Virginia is known for coal mining, but it's also famous for salt mines. Appalachian salt has won taste tests around the world! Before refrigeration, salt was key for curing (another way of preserving) hunts and harvests. A family could butcher a pig in fall and eat salt pork all winter. Salt is also essential for turning cabbage into sauerkraut. And it's the namesake ingredient in Appalachia's famous salt-rising bread.

GREASY BEANS

"Greasy beans" aren't really greasy—
they're a shiny, smooth type of green
bean beloved in Appalachia!

CHICKEN AND DUMPLINGS

Boiled dumplings, called "slickers," are rolled
out flat and served with chicken. Sometimes,
the beloved dinner is known as "chicken slick."

GOLDEN DELICIOUS APPLE

The Golden Delicious apple
was discovered on a hillside
farm in 1912. It's now the
official state fruit.

CHARLESTON
★

PEPPERONI ROLL

The pepperoni roll, made of soft bread
dough with pepperoni baked in the
middle, began as a portable meal
for Italian coal miners in the 1930s.
People still love it today.

LEATHER BRITCHES

Before refrigerators were
available, West Virginians
made "leather britches"
from fresh green beans.
The beans were strung on
thread, hung, and dried, to
be added to soups all winter.

SALT

West Virginia's award-winning
salt has been produced in
the small town of Malden for
more than 200 years.

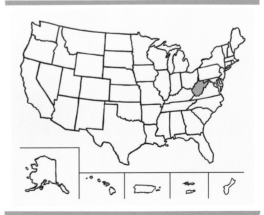

Succotash

PREPARATION TIME	COOKING TIME	LEVEL OF DIFFICULTY	SERVES
10 minutes	20 minutes	● ○ ○	4–6

The word "succotash" comes from Narragansett word *sohquttahhash*, or "broken corn kernels." This side dish of sweet corn and creamy lima beans can be dressed up with red and green bell peppers, both of which are plentiful in Southern gardens in summer. Some families also like succotash with their Thanksgiving turkey.

INGREDIENTS

2 tablespoons olive oil
1 sweet onion, finely chopped
3 cups corn kernels (from about 3 ears)
1½ cups cherry tomatoes, halved
2 cups canned lima beans, drained and rinsed
¾ cup chicken stock, preferably low-sodium
3 tablespoons butter, cut into pieces
1 tablespoon fresh lemon juice
1 tablespoon plus 1 teaspoon chopped fresh flat-leaf parsley
¾ teaspoon salt
½ teaspoon freshly ground black pepper

1. In a cast-iron skillet, heat the oil over medium heat. Add the onion and cook, stirring occasionally, until softened and translucent, about 5 minutes.

2. Stir in the corn and cook, stirring frequently, until tender, about 6 minutes.

3. Stir in the tomatoes, lima beans, and stock, and simmer until the tomatoes start to break down, 3–5 minutes.

4. Remove from the heat and stir in the butter, lemon juice, parsley, salt, and pepper. Serve.

Eating in WISCO

There's a good reason why Wisconsin is called America's Dairyland. Cows here produce an average of 2.6 *billion* pounds of milk per month! Some of that milk goes into cartons for pouring into glasses and over bowls of cereal, but lots of it will get made into Wisconsin's most famous food: cheese.

Swiss immigrants brought cheesemaking to Wisconsin in the 1800s, using copper kettles to turn milk into something that could last for weeks, months, or even years. Today, Wisconsin makes more cheese than any other state—more than three billion pounds each year! The hundreds of varieties include strong-smelling Limburger, creamy mozzarella, salty feta, and crumbly Mexican *cotija*.

Wisconsinites top their burgers with cheese, but here in Dairyland, they slather butter on top, too, for a treat called the "butter burger." They brush bratwurst with melted butter. Some dairies make cheese-filled sausages called cheddarwurst—try them at the state fair.

At bitter cold Green Bay Packers football games, you'll see lots of fans (known as Cheeseheads) proudly wearing orange hats that look like giant wedges of Wisconsin cheese.

SAUSAGES

German and Polish immigrants brought sausages including bratwurst and kielbasa to Wisconsin.

CHEESE CURDS

These squeak when you eat them.

FISH FRY

The Friday night fish fry is a beloved Wisconsin tradition. Fresh fish caught in the Great Lakes, like perch or walleye, are usually on the menu.

BOOYAH STEW

At community events, giant "booyah" stews are cooked in iron kettles that can hold more than 50 gallons. People yell "Booyah" when the stew is ready to eat.

MADISON ★

CRANBERRIES

Wisconsin farmers grow more than half of America's cranberries in giant wetlands called bogs.

FROZEN CUSTARD

Wisconsin's frozen custard is richer and thicker than ice cream.

MADISON FARMERS' MARKET

The Dane County Farmers' Market, next to the state capitol building in Madison, is one of the most famous in the whole country.

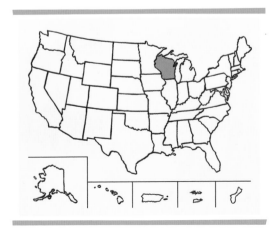

Stovetop Macaroni and Cheese

PREPARATION TIME	COOKING TIME	LEVEL OF DIFFICULTY	SERVES
10 minutes	10 minutes	● ● ○	2–4

Kiss the orange powder packet good-bye! Once you try the rich, creamy goodness of homemade cheese sauce on your mac, you'll take the extra moment to whip it up from scratch while the water's boiling. Thanks to the state's many master cheese makers, Wisconsin cheddar is an excellent choice.

INGREDIENTS

Coarse salt

8 ounces elbow macaroni

½ cup sour cream

2 tablespoons unsalted butter

1 teaspoon Dijon mustard

8 ounces cheddar cheese, grated (about 2 packed cups)

Pinch of cayenne pepper (optional)

1. Bring a medium pot of water to a boil over high heat and add salt to the water. Cook the macaroni until just al dente, about 8 minutes. Drain well.

2. Return the pot to medium heat and add the sour cream and butter. Stir quickly until the butter is melted, then stir in the mustard followed by the cheese. Continue stirring quickly until the cheese is melted and a smooth, creamy sauce forms, about 2 minutes. Season with salt and a pinch of cayenne, if desired. Add the macaroni and stir until it's coated with the cheese sauce. Serve immediately.

Eating in WYOM[ING]

Wyoming has the fewest people of any state, which leaves lots of land for riding horses. It's known as the Cowboy State, and you'll find real-life cowboys here—and cowgirls, too. In fact, Wyoming's other nickname is the Equality State, because it was the first territory where women won the right to vote. Yahoo!

The spectacular Grand Teton Mountains draw brave tourists and athletes who climb to its snow-capped peaks. Yellowstone, the world's first national park, is famous for geysers, hot springs, and dramatic rock formations, along with elk, bears, bison, antelope, and sheep. All these animals are delicious to eat, though in Yellowstone, only the wolves are allowed to do so. People in Wyoming do hunt and eat lots of game—*outside* the park.

Cattle cover Wyoming's vast ranches, and rodeos are the official state sport. Visitors to Cheyenne's annual Frontier Days begin their swashbuckling mornings with 500 gallons of coffee and 100,000 pancakes! If you consider yourself a cowboy- or cowgirl-in-training, you can work up an appetite in a cattle drive at a dude ranch. For dinner, sit down for a cowboy-style meal of prime beef, elk steak, bison steak, or beef chili. Save room for cowboy cookies, named for their large size and hearty ingredients!

MILK CAN SUPPER

Milk can supper is a stew of sausage, potatoes, and other vegetables, combined in a big metal milk can and cooked over a campfire.

BARLEY

Wyoming and its Rocky Mountain neighbors lead the nation in barley production. Some of it is turned into sweet drinks, like chocolate malts.

JERKY

Dried elk, bison, and beef jerky still offer a taste the Wild West, whether you ride a horse or a bicycle.

WYOMING JERKY

BEEF

CHEYENNE

ELK

Wyoming game hunters cook elk meat into burgers, chili, steaks, or stews such as Elk Burgundy.

BROWN BEANS

Authentic ranch cuisine is still alive today. Groups compete in cooking contests using chuck wagon ingredients that include beans and cured meats.

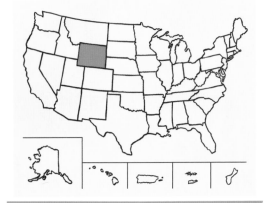

229

Bison Burgers

PREPARATION TIME	COOKING TIME	LEVEL OF DIFFICULTY	SERVES
5 minutes	10 minutes	● ○ ○	4

America was once covered with herds of bison. Twenty to thirty million of the giant mammals roamed the prairies and plains. They nearly went extinct in the 1800s, when many were hunted for just one part: their delicious giant tongues! Today, bison are raised on farms and people use the whole animal. Ground bison makes a very delicious burger and is available in supermarkets all over the country. If you can't find it, substitute any ground meat in this recipe.

INGREDIENTS
1½ pounds ground bison
   (or lean ground beef)
1 teaspoon coarse salt
1 tablespoon butter
1 tablespoon vegetable oil
4 burger buns, split and
   lightly toasted
Ketchup, mayonnaise, and
   sliced pickles, for serving

1. Dividing evenly, gently form the ground bison into 4 patties, each about 1 inch thick, and transfer to a plate. Season patties on one side with half the salt, dividing evenly.

2. In a large, heavy skillet, such as cast-iron, heat butter and oil over medium. When butter is melted and skillet is hot, add the patties, seasoned sides down. Season the tops with the remaining ½ teaspoon salt, and cook until the bottoms are nicely browned, about 5 minutes. Flip and cook for 3 to 4 minutes longer for medium burgers.

3. Sandwich burgers in toasted buns and serve immediately, with ketchup, mayonnaise, and pickles.

RECIPE INDEX BY LEVEL OF DIFFICULTY

INDEX

RECIPE NOTES

Here are a few good rules of thumb to keep in mind when shopping and cooking. Unless a recipe says otherwise, we use:

- Unsalted butter
- Coarse salt and freshly ground pepper
- Fresh herbs, including flat-leaf (not curly) parsley
- Large eggs
- Whole milk
- Large garlic cloves (use two if yours are small)

MEASUREMENT NOTES

- All spoon and cup measurements are level.
- 1 teaspoon = 5 ml; 1 tablespoon = 15 ml.
- Cooking and preparation times are for guidance, but individual ovens may vary, so check for doneness. If using a convection (fan), follow manufacturer's instructions.
- When a recipe doesn't specify an exact amount—like when drizzling oil, seasoning with salt and pepper, garnishing with fresh herbs, or sprinkling with powdered sugar to finish a dish—the quantities are flexible. Use the photograph—and your taste—as guides.

NOTE ON SAFETY

This book and the recipes presented in this book are designed for children but assume adult supervision at all times. Although we take care to identify any hazards, we do not take any responsibility for your children during the preparation and cooking of these dishes, or for any adverse reactions to ingredients or finished dishes. It is up to parents and caregivers to choose appropriate recipes and ingredients and to ensure the safety of the children under their supervision.

Phaidon Press Inc.
65 Bleecker Street
New York, NY 10012

Phaidon Press Limited
Regent's Wharf
All Saints Street
London N1 9PA

phaidon.com

First published 2019
© 2019 Phaidon Press Limited
Text copyright Gabrielle Langholtz © 2019
Illustrations copyright Jenny Bowers © 2019
Typeset in Alinea and TT Nooks

ISBN 978 0 7148 7862 1
002 – 0319

Designed by Meagan Bennett
Photographs by Danielle Acken
Project Edited by Ellen Morrissey

Printed in China